TRAV
SE

"Informative and fun. Includes places off the beaten track." -K

Travel Like a Local Chicago: Chicago Illinois Travel Guide by Nora Willi

"Best guide book to get the true local intel of how to navigate and spend your time in Denver. From food to experiences to outdoor activities and everything in between, Taylor gives the reader a list of incredible options to choose from that fits their desires. I especially love her hints on traveling sustainably!" - Lexi K.

Travel Like a Local Denver : Denver Colorado Travel Guide by Taylor Norberg

"An excellent resource for getting the lowdown on Las Vegas. It is a great tool for anyone visiting Vegas to have in their back pocket to make your visit more pleasant. The author did a great job of capturing the essence of Las Vegas." -Andrew D.

Travel Like a Local Las Vegas : Las Vegas Nevada Travel Guide by Tessa Holden

For this audiobook, free audiobooks,
& free travel tools.

TRAVEL LIKE A LOCAL-PERTH

Perth Australia Travel Guide

Janet Daniels-Thomas

Travel Like a Local Perth Copyright © 2024 by CZYK Publishing LLC. All Rights Reserved.

All rights reserved. No part of this book may be reproduced in any form or by any electronic or mechanical means including information storage and retrieval systems, without permission in writing from the author. The only exception is by a reviewer, who may quote short excerpts in a review.

The statements in this book are of the authors and may not be the views of CZYK Publishing or Greater Than a Tourist.

First Edition

Cover designed by: Ivana Stamenkovic

Cover Image: https://pixabay.com/photos/perth-kings-park-australia-744266/

CZYK PUBLISHING

CZYK Publishing Since 2011.
CZYKPublishing.com
Travel Like a Local

Mill Hall, PA
All rights reserved.

Travel Like a Local

METRIC CONVERSIONS

TEMPERATURE

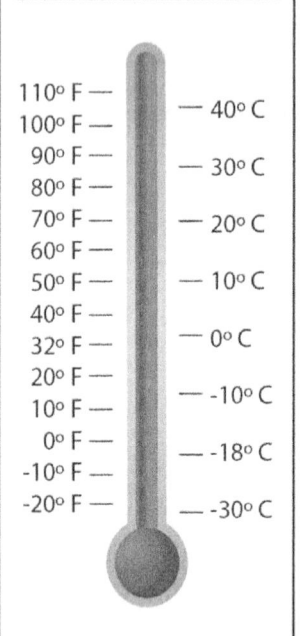

110° F — — 40° C
100° F —
90° F — — 30° C
80° F —
70° F — — 20° C
60° F —
50° F — — 10° C
40° F —
32° F — — 0° C
20° F —
10° F — — -10° C
0° F —
-10° F — — -18° C
-20° F — — -30° C

To convert F to C:
Subtract 32, and then multiply by 5/9 or .5555.

To Convert C to F:
Multiply by 1.8 and then add 32.

32F = 0C

LIQUID VOLUME

To Convert:	Multiply by
U.S. Gallons to Liters	3.8
U.S. Liters to Gallons	.26
Imperial Gallons to U.S. Gallons	1.2
Imperial Gallons to Liters	4.55
Liters to Imperial Gallons	.22

1 Liter = .26 U.S. Gallon
1 U.S. Gallon = 3.8 Liters

DISTANCE

To convert	Multiply by
Inches to Centimeters	2.54
Centimeters to Inches	.39
Feet to Meters	.3
Meters to Feet	3.28
Yards to Meters	.91
Meters to Yards	1.09
Miles to Kilometers	1.61
Kilometers to Miles	.62

1 Mile = 1.6 km
1 km = .62 Miles

WEIGHT

1 Ounce = .28 Grams
1 Pound = .4555 Kilograms
1 Gram = .04 Ounce
1 Kilogram = 2.2 Pounds

BOOK DESCRIPTION

Travel Like a Local is a series of travel guidebooks written by local experts to help travelers explore new places like an insider. From learning about the culture and customs to finding the best restaurants and attractions, these guidebooks provide comprehensive information to ensure a hassle-free unforgettable journey. Each guidebook is packed with insider tips and recommendations, tailored specifically to the location, so you can make the most of your time and truly get to know the destination. With The Travel Like a Local Guidebooks you'll get the most out of your travels.

OUR STORY

Traveling is a passion of Travel Like a Local book series creator. Lisa studied abroad in college, and for their honeymoon Lisa and her husband toured Europe. During her travels to Malta, an older man tried to give her some advice based on his own experience living on the island since he was a young boy. She was not sure if she should talk to the stranger but was interested in his advice. When traveling to some places she was wary to talk to locals because she was afraid that they weren't being genuine. Through her travels, Lisa learned how much locals had to share with tourists. Lisa created the Travel Like a Local book series to help connect people with locals. A topic that locals are very passionate about sharing.

TABLE OF CONTENTS

Travel Like a Local

1. Things to pack for a visit to Perth
2. Perth, Western Australia: A Brief Overview
3. Perth's History
4. Staying Safe around Snakes, Spiders and Sharks
5. Emergency Numbers and Perth's Hospitals
6. Local Newspapers and Social Media
7. Local Groceries and Snacks
8. Safety Tips as you travel Perth
9. Perth Culture
10. Getting around Perth – Public Transport
11. Where to Rent Cars
12. Bougee Places to stay
13. "Yeah, I can spend a bit" places to stay
14. Affordable Places - Kangaroo INN
15. Affordable Places - Spinners BACKPACKERS (Northbridge)
16. Affordable Places - Beatty LODGE (Leederville)
17. Affordable Places - Downtown BACKPACKERS HOSTEL
18. Affordable Places - Sprials BACKPACKERS (Northbridge)
19. Perth's most posh places to eat
20. Smash a meal with the Locals

21. Travelling Solo
22. Romantic Couples Activities to do
23. Family Friendly Activities - Scitech
24. Take the Family to Hillary's Harbor
25. Take the family to "Aqwa" Aquarium
26. Family friendly Adventure World Theme Park
27. Family friendly Waterslides at Outback Splash
28. Rottnest "Wadjemup" ISLAND
29. City of Perth Zoo
30. City of Perth's Museum
31. City of Perth's Art Gallery
32. Day Trippin' - Rockingham
33. Day Trippin' – Swan Valley: Whiteman Park, Wine & Beer Tours
34. Day Trippin' – Mandurah: The Mandurah Giants.
35. Day Trippin' – Fremantle: Freo Markets & Island Hopping
36. Day Trippin Rockingham Penguin Island
37. Weekend Roadtrip – call shotgun on the way to Bussleton
38. Weekend Roadtrip – call shotgun on the way to Margaret River
39. Weekend Roadtrip – call shotgun on the long drive down to Albany – via Pemberton

40. Adventures you need a week to see. Maybe a plane, too
41. Perth's Night Fever Nightlife
42. "Sweet, Bro" Perth's tastiest desserts
43. Perth's Prettiest Pubs
44. "Beach me off" - Scarborough Beach
45. "Beach me off" – Cottesloe Beach
46. "Beach me off" – City & Trigg Beaches
47. "Beach me off" – Coogee Beach
48. Strip it Down – Perth's Nudist Beaches
49. Take a drive along Perth's Amazing Coastline
50. "Time to go" – Ideas for Gifts to take home with you that are unique to Perth

References:

DEDICATION

To my gorgeous husband Alun; who makes every journey so much fun – whether it's to Koh Samui or the local grocery store.

ABOUT THE AUTHOR

Janet is 46 and has lived in Perth, Western Australia for over 25 years. Janet is happily married and has a passion for writing.

HOW TO USE THIS BOOK

Welcome to the Travel Like a Local Guidebook series! Our mission is to give readers an inside look at travel destinations around the world through the eyes of locals. Each guidebook in this series is written by a local who has explored and experienced the destination in depth. The author has made suggestions based on their own experiences. Please check before traveling to the area in case the suggested places are unavailable.

Travel Advisories: As a first step in planning any trip abroad, check the Travel Advisories for your intended destination.
https://travel.state.gov/content/travel/en/traveladvisories/traveladvisories.html

FROM THE PUBLISHER

Traveling can be one of the most important parts of a person's life. The anticipation and memories that you have are some of the best. As a publisher of the Travel Like a Local, Greater Than a Tourist, East Like a Local, as well as the popular *50 Things to Know* book series, we strive to help you learn about new places, spark your imagination, and inspire you. Wherever you are and whatever you do I wish you safe, fun, and inspiring travel.

Lisa Rusczyk Ed. D.
CZYK Publishing

TRAVEL LIKE A LOCAL

Travel Like a Local

Pack your bags, we're going to Perth, Western Australia. *Holidays*. Even just the word makes me smile. If you're planning to come to Perth for a visit, you've picked what I think is the prettiest city in Australia. You'll be excited for coming to see and sample Perth's best and brightest offerings, so I want to help you prepare for your best holiday ever.

1. THINGS TO PACK FOR A VISIT TO PERTH

Sun cream – *vital* in our Perth heat.

Season-appropriate clothing. Perth has amazing winters which we locals think is really cold and wet, but people from the East Coast think it's not cold at all. With that in mind, I recommend bringing clothes for mostly summer (shorts, summer dresses, cool, breathable cotton t-shirts), but pack a pair of jeans and a few jackets, warm socks and warm pjs if you're coming in the winter. Check out Perth's weather before you arrive so you know what to wear for the most comfort.

Some closed-in shoes; these will protect your feet from being exposed to our mozzies and small critters.

If you're here with goals to hike/go on long walks, pack walking/hiking shoes to keep your feet comfortable on those long journeys, it makes such a difference.

If you're coming over from Interstate, we're a fairly warm climate city, so bring a lot of cool, breathable clothing, bring comfortable footwear.

Bring some insect repellent – or you can buy some when you arrive in Perth, but it's always handy to keep some on you.

Medications you regularly take – super important to have these handy.

A small first aid kit – because you just never know.

Ear plugs and eye masks – even in a posh hotel, there could be a concert nearby and you want to get the best rest you can.

Swimwear and thongs (flip-flops – we call them 'thongs') for the beach.

The "Smarter Travel" website (2023) recommends bringing a light jacket with you (it can get quite chilly of an evening during spring and autumn) as well as a small bag or backpack for when you're travelling about.

Travel Like a Local

Not really something to pack, but definitely sort some travel insurance out – make sure you're covered for emergencies when you're far from home, you know?

2. PERTH, WESTERN AUSTRALIA: A BRIEF OVERVIEW

G'day and welcome to the land of the "sandgropers". Other Aussies call us Perth people *sandgropers* because we live so close to the coast and everywhere we go is covered in fine white sand – even our footpaths. You're about to embark on the best holiday ever – in the city of Light. Yep, way back in 1962, Perth residents and businesses left on their lights, shone torches to the sky and lit lanterns to generate as much light as possible – an Astronaut commented on the brightness from space and *Perth became known as The City of Light.*

Here in the gorgeous city of Perth, we're super lucky to have over 280 days of sunshine in the year. Although we go through 4 seasons, even our winters can be sunny and bright. *Every* season gives travellers and locals so many opportunities to be out and about; not hindered by the weather.

You're at the heart of Western Australia in what I – a local – consider to be the prettiest city in the world. We're not a huge city (there's almost 2 million of us in Perth but considering Perth is the same size as Singapore -which has 6 million in population – that should give you a bit of insight as to how 'little' Perth is). We're not a huge city, but omg we are a *gorgeous* place to live in or visit. We have the prettiest buildings, the nicest people and the most pristine beaches.

Perth has a sunny, bright Mediterranean-style (so, fairly warm) climate throughout the year with an average of about eight hours of sunshine per day – even in winter.

Summers are hot and Perth has a really *dry heat* (we don't sweat, we cook slowly in the sun!), so I recommend investing in a great sunscreen with at least SPF factor of 30 to keep your skin protected if you're traveling about during the hot seasons. Our summers feel the hottest at the beginning of the year, then cool down to winter temperatures of between 15-23 degrees during July and August. Winters are cool and wet (but most days are still pretty sunny), with most of Perth's annual rainfall falling between May and September. Spring is probably the best time to visit, with warm and clear conditions and a brilliant display of gorgeous wildflowers throughout Western Australia.

3. PERTH'S HISTORY

We're a city of perfect blue buildings, bright skies and a mix of historical structures and brand-new glass skyscrapers.

Perth was named after the city of Perth in Scotland and was founded by Captain James Stirling in 1829. The National Museum of Australia (2023) states: *"Perth was founded by Captain James Stirling on Whadjuk country as the capital of the Swan River Colony in 1829. It was the first free-settler colony in Australia established by private capital. From 1850, convicts began to arrive at the colony in large numbers to build roads and other public infrastructure."* Perth acquired 'city status' in 1856 and has been a city of constant growth, change and beauty ever since.

^^ Author's photo of Perth's bustling city centre in the middle of summer. The contrast between historical buildings from the 1800's and the new, shiny buildings of the past 10-15 years make the gorgeous topography of Perth CBD (Central Business District) one of the prettiest and most interesting ones I've ever seen.

Travel Like a Local

For more information about Perth, I recommend a quick visit to *The Western Australian Visitor Centre* located at: 55 William Street (Perth CBD). Helpful staff there can assist with everything to help you enjoy your holiday. They can book accommodation or tours and also have a wide selection of brochures on places of interest throughout the state. Give them a call on: **9483 1111**. They're open 7 days, so you can pop in to see the guys or you can check out what's on offer through their website: www.wavisitorcentre.com.au

4. STAYING SAFE AROUND SNAKES, SPIDERS AND SHARKS

Staying safe from Perth's dangerous critters. Keep an eye out on your Perth visit for our "big 3" – snakes, spiders and sharks.

Snakes. Here in Perth we're aware of dugites (brown snakes) in our long grasses and heavily dense environments. Dugites are poisonous and can cause a lot of pain *or even death* if you get bitten, so please stay on footpaths and closest to communal areas rather than wandering "out back". The Snake Catcher Perth website (2023) warns: *"There are two primary species of snakes encountered in the Perth metro area. These are Dugites and Tiger Snakes. Both of these species are DANGEROUSLY VENOMOUS, which means* *envenomation is potentially fatal without medical assistance.*" Areas where dugites/other snakes have been spotted are usually sign posted, but to keep yourself safe, please stick to clear areas for tourist exploration.

Spiders. Generally these little critters like to stay hidden and probably won't bother you if you don't bother them, but in case of any curious bites, it's important to get yourself to the hospital as quickly as you can. If you do get bitten, try to record as much as you can about the type of spider that got you so that medical staff know exactly how to help you.

Sharks. I'm of the opinion that once we go into the sea, we're on *their* turf. Do everything you can to keep yourself safe by not going out too far once you're in the water. Stay within the marked flags and if you're not a confident swimmer, definitely stick to the shallows. We have some awesome Lifeguards on duty at every beach but if you're hanging out ocean-side outside of lifeguard hours, try not to go swimming or surfing at sunrise or around dusk as these are the times we have the most reported shark sightings.

Travel Like a Local

5. EMERGENCY NUMBERS AND PERTH'S HOSPITALS

For International Travellers visiting Perth, there are 10 consulate generals in Perth and 48 consulates; these include consulates for countries such as Austria, Canada, Brazil, Germany, Hungary, New Zealand, Poland and Mauritius. Consulates and consulate generals are there to help you in times of emergency, such as when a passport has been lost or stolen, or to provide advice and support in the case of an accident, serious illness or death.

For all emergencies, we all call "**000**" to contact Police or Ambulances immediately. Try to stay calm, explain in as much detail as you can about what has happened and know that our Police and Ambos will be doing everything they can to help you as quickly as possible.

For emergencies, these are the best Hospitals to get yourself to:

Royal Perth Hospital – situated right in the City Center – including the State Major Trauma Center. This is by far the best hospital in Perth, but I'm a little biased because my husband is a Senior Nurse at the Emergency ward.

PCH – Perth Children's Hospital

Fiona Stanley Hospital – burns specialists.

Sir Charles Gairdner

Joondalup Peel Health Campus

Midland Hospital/St John of God

St John Urgent Care – various locations across the city for when it's not an emergency but is still pretty bad and needs medical attention.

6. LOCAL NEWSPAPERS AND SOCIAL MEDIA

"*Perth Now*" is our local newspaper with news on community events, upcoming concerts and things like that.

We locals like to refer to the "*Perth is OK*" website (https://perthisok.com/) for daily updates on what's going on around our gorgeous city. 'Perth is OK' lets us know of upcoming events, cool places to eat, new adventures to try and gives up-to-the-minute Perth news so you'll have your hand on the Perth pulse and know the best festivals to attend, the popular places to hang and the most recent (therefore coolest) places open to grab a bite or try new cocktails with your mates.

Take pics of your awesome holiday and upload them on Insta; tagging "#PerthIsOk" on your posts so your gorgeous trip will be shared across thousands of sites.

7. LOCAL GROCERIES AND SNACKS

It's fun to eat out on holidays but for every meal over a long period, it starts to cut into the holiday expenses a lot. Here are places we locals go to get our groceries and snacks on a budget:

Coles
Woolworths ("*Woolies*")
At a pinch, IGA stock groceries too.

Sometimes the IGA stores are called "*The Good Grocers*" which means it's a bougee version of IGA. These 'good grocers' have fancy biscuits, pretty floral posies, the highest (and most expensive) cuts of the finest meats and have ready-made bougee platters for buying and impressing guests with at parties. These IGA/Good Grocery places are pricier than our local Supermarkets, but they have longer hours of operation than Woolworths and Coles and are fairly convenient to access – especially on public holidays when pretty much the whole city shuts down.

Pretty much every suburb in Perth has a town center and that's where you'll find the daily grocery supplies you'll need.

For amazing snacks, we have some really great Asian-inspired 'supermarkets' dotted around Perth – especially throughout Northbridge. You can pop in and get funky packets of Asian lollies, noodles, take-home dumplings or brightly coloured packets of chips/crisps with big

cartoon or manga-inspired graphics. Northbridge also has an American-based snacks store along Newcastle Street which sells American cereals, "twinkies" (omg those are so good, you guys), American sodas and even have machines where you can fill up with your favourite brightly-coloured, sugar-loaded 'slurpies'.

8. SAFETY TIPS AS YOU TRAVEL PERTH

Be sun safe – **wear a hat**. Try to get a wide-brimmed hat that covers your face, shoulders and neck or at least something that covers as much as your face as you can. **Put sun cream on** the back of your neck and ears to help keep them protected during the hot summer months.

Stay hydrated – keep a bottle of water with you at all times.

The hottest parts of the day are between 11am – 3pm, so be mindful of this while you're out and about and try to stay in shady areas. Be aware of animals and stay clear of them if you see snakes or spiders. We have

Quokkas on Rottnest and Quintas (they look a lot like the Quokkas at Rotto, but are only found in specific places) at Victoria Gardens in East Perth.

9. PERTH CULTURE

You might not notice it right away, but there's a definite lasting (friendly, but) rivalry throughout Perth; between the North Perth 'city folk' and the 'laid-back Southerners'. We tease each other and we compete with each other but at the end of the day, we're all from Perth and passionate about the city we live in. South of Perth peeps think we Northerners are too posh and too into materialistic things. We think people South of the river are country bumpkins. They even dress differently in dyed shirts, torn denim jeans and sandals. As a city girl, I love being part of the more Cosmopolitan part of Perth. It's definitely a shift travelling to South Perth. Going to Fremantle, for instance – you'll notice the cars are much older and drive a lot slower. Freo people are usually floating about on scooters or bikes – or walking everywhere - and they seem to take life at a much slower pace to the city folk North of Perth.

The Swan River cuts east to west through the middle of metropolitan Perth and is the defining line between North and South Perth, serving as our measurement for whether a person sides with to the busy city folk or the chilled-out southerners. Northerners will tell you they have better beaches, are better connected, and have better nightlife options. A southerner will defend their laid-back lifestyle and beautiful riverfronts.

Our 2 beloved Perth AFL teams are The West Coast Eagles and The Fremantle Dockers. Pick a side because you won't get away with liking both equally. Haha.

Perth is known as a *quiet* city because (as far as I know, anyway) our nightlife isn't as exciting as the Eastern States. Our stores close at 5pm sharp on weekdays, so make sure you get any groceries before then or you'll find yourself empty-handed otherwise. We have pubs and clubs that come to life on Friday nights and over the weekend. A quick search on "Perth is OK" will alert you to live bands, comedy sessions, great pubs with new meals to try out or any cool Festivals (we love our yearly "Fringe Festival") you can buy tickets to go and see. Once a year – around October I think – we hold the Perth Royal Show on the Claremont showgrounds. We have special trainlines set aside to take tens of thousands to the show. Be prepared to spend like an unsupervised 8-year-old on the many

Travel Like a Local

showbags, balls of fairy floss, a good old "sausage on a stick" or curly fries in cones of newspaper pages. The show is a huge event and loads of fun to go to. I highly recommend attending, but set yourself a spending limit or you'll come home not knowing where a cool thousand went.

10. GETTING AROUND PERTH – PUBLIC TRANSPORT

We offer great public transport options on our trains, buses or ferries. Transperth is the company that oversees all tickets and public transport travel here in Perth and if you're thinking of staying a while and saving the costs of booking a car, you'll need to get yourself a ***Smartrider travel card***. You can pop into the main Transperth office in the main Train Station at Perth's Central Business District (CBD), fill out a form, add some credit and off you go – ready to catch trains, buses and even try the ferry to South Perth at your leisure.

To get hold of a *SmartRider* card in the city, they can be purchased at Transperth InfoCentres located at the Elizabeth Quay Bus Station, Perth Busport, Perth Station or Perth Underground. More than 60 retail outlets also sell *SmartRider* cards. The only downside is that *SmartRider* cards can't be bought online, they have to be bought in person.

Our free"CAT" (Central Area Transit) Buses are free, clean, comfortable buses that follow large loops based around the city centre.

Travel Like a Local

Each Cat Bus includes tourist stops in their travel loop, so these are a great idea to catch and get a great free bus tour of Perth's most popular places. The Red Cat loops around the city centre's main malls and off to West Perth where businesses and Perth's finest bakeries live. The Blue Cat takes passengers around the Northbridge area and down to Elizabeth Quays. The Yellow Cat takes you to Royal Perth Hospital and down to East Perth – one of Perth's most stunning suburbs with beautiful Victoria Gardens and the pretty by-the-river cafes and restaurants. The Green Cat goes to Kings Park which is absolutely beautiful – filled with wildflowers and an incredible view from the entrance over the Perth skyline. We Locals love watching our yearly Australia Day fireworks either from Kings Park or Langley Park which is closer to the river and not on a hill. A new Cat bus – the purple bus – takes passengers to the hospitals south of the River.

Alternatively, you can download the right apps and hire an eScooter to get around Perth's main city centres – Perth CBD, Fremantle and Mandurah all have eScooters dotted around which are easy to use. Please wear the helmets that come attached, they may save your life.

11. WHERE TO RENT CARS

"*No Birds*" Car Rental are the most popular when it comes to renting your own vehicle while travelling Perth. You'll legit see their white cars with their recognisable 'no birds' sticker *everywhere*. They offer great prices and packages and have offices at the Airport so you can hop straight into your own car from the plane and drop it off before you board the flight home. Easy, right?

Alternatively, here are other Car Rental companies in Perth:
- Perth Rent-a-Car
- Hertz
- Budget Car Rental

Travel Like a Local

PERTH ACCOMODATION FROM BOUGEE TO BACKPACKERS

12. BOUGEE PLACES TO STAY

I mean, come on - let's start our accommodation recommendations with Perth's most glamorous places. Am I right? As a 'city girl', I love me a 5-star stay in *luxury* place to stay. I'll even go camping – as long as the tent is *a Glamping tent* fitted with a luxurious Queen-sized bed and covered with 1000-threadcount Egyptian cotton. Just saying.

If you've got a full bank account, these are the 'high roller' hotels I highly recommend. These places are bougee AF:

ROLLIN' AT CROWN CASINO.

Not gonna lie, I've not actually stayed at the Crown. I'd *like* to, I just haven't given it a shot, yet. One day! It's probably one of the most expensive places to stay, but the rooms are *fire*, and the grounds are meticulously kept.

I've heard loads of great things about staying at the Crown from all my mates, though. They say the rooms are absolutely gorgeous, spacious and really beautifully decorated. I've seen photos online of the bathrooms and they look so pretty (I don't know about you, but the hotel room's shower is a winner for me. A good one and I'm all in). The rooms look well appointed and the pool area for guests is vast, clear, sparkling and blue.

All my boxes are ticked. Awesome.

I highly recommend even *one night's stay* here just to experience it – and try your luck at the casino while you're at it with a plethora of awesome places to eat.

Nobu for example - a highly praised Restaurant at the Casino has won awards for its fine dining experience and has amazing Japanese-style dishes. I personally prefer going to

The Merrywell for wholesome, delicious "pub style" meals – including the *best* nachos in the whole of WA. I'm not even joking. Those nachos *will* change your life. The *Merrywell* does huge servings of all their pub-friendly meals so if you order the nachos, make sure you have 2-3 mates to help you eat it, it's a literal mountain of nachos with an insane (yet delicious) amount of cheese, meat and all the other yummy things that make nachos the awesome meal they are.

LUX LIVING AT FRASER SUITES, EAST PERTH.

So okay...I've not stayed in these gorgeous apartments *either*, but the photos of the suites on the internet are *incredible*. For square footage of each gigantic, plush room alone, it's worth the price. **You'll feel like royalty in these suites**. I've had friends who have stayed here and rave about how amazing it is.

This is lux living at its very best. The apartments are a great combination of feeling right at home (you can cook your own meals if you really want to) yet also getting daily maid service. I work right by Fraser Suites, and I'd say the only downfall is not being able to access a cheap grocery store easily. They've recently opened a new IGA store only 2 minutes' walk from the Fraser Suites, but everything there (while looking absolutely beautiful) is expensive, so you'll have to weigh up how much you want that bag of chips/fruit salad. I'd recommend getting your shopping done in the city as it's cheaper than having to buy food from nearby cafes or from the newly opened East Perth IGA – they have beautiful things, but all at a cost. Get yo' snacks from Coles or Woolies in the city centre and beat the high prices.

EST, RELAX AND RESET AT HIDDEN VALLEY FOREST RETREAT.

My husband and I have had the pleasure of 3 different occasions where we've stayed here, and *this is my favourite holiday destination in the whole of Western Australia.*

If I could give this incredible place *more* stars out of 5, I would. It's the most magical, restful, natural, eco-friendly and yet *luxe* place my husband and I have ever stayed in.

Travel Like a Local

There are 4 different Eco-Villas to rent, but we went all out with "*Deepriver Lodge*" – our own eco 'resort style' house *with our very own lake* to paddleboard or canoe in. Excellent. Situated in lush Western Australia forest, you can expect to see some kangaroos at dusk and hear all kinds of birds happily chirping throughout the day.

Deep river Lodge has 4-5 stunning, natural 'seating' areas – one with a deep tub to relax in with their house-made wines and a cheese plate.

All photos of **Hidden Valley Forest Retreat** are from the Author's stay with her husband over 3 separate visits to the "*Deepriver Lodge*".

Tim and Lily at Hidden Valley Retreat (it should be called a *Resort*, honestly) will stop at nothing to make you feel welcome, comfortable and spoilt on your entire stay. Lily will make a gorgeous platter of local foods, wines and cheeses for dinner and Tim is happy to tell you about all the local attractions. Alun and I stayed each time during winter and were so blessed to come back from walking in the woods to see the wood fire had been set for us and fresh wood had been cut and stacked by the front door for our use. We loved sitting by our own lake (*I mean, come on now – if that's not luxury, I don't know what is*!) and taking a rainfall/waterfall shower in the *nicest* bathroom I've ever encountered. From the thoughtful freshly picked flowers placed on the dinner and coffee tables to the gorgeous hands-picked bathroom items (soaps, shampoos) along with the lush forest and spotting all kinds of native animals and wildflowers, we couldn't want anything more.

The Pullman – Bunker Bay, WA.

If you're heading down south for a long weekend, this is the place to stay. The *All Accor* (2023) Luxury Stays website says the following about staying at *The Pullman, Bunker Bay*: "Just over three hour's drive south of Perth,

Travel Like a Local

Pullman Bunker Bay Resort offers the ultimate getaway. Nestled on the white sands of Bunker Bay, our 5-star Margaret River Region resort boasts an absolute beachfront location with direct beach access. Guests can relax, recharge & unwind. Look to explore the surrounding area including nearby Dunsborough, Yallingup and the amazing Margaret River wine region. Avid scuba divers cannot miss the beautiful Geographe Bay, just an hour from our Margaret River resort. With an amazing beachfront location, Pullman Bunker Bay Resort Margaret River is the ideal getaway destination. With Bunker Bay beach on the doorstep and Geographe Bay and the Margaret River wine region a short distance away, guests can indulge and relax".

Baller "Glamping" at Discovery Village – Rottnest Island.

When it comes to camping *clears throat*, I prefer somewhere with a fully installed bathroom and a luxury bedroom (with a proper bed in it – no puffy air mattress for me, sir!) with direct beach access, *am I right?*

My husband and I checked out Rottnest's finest glamping tent last winter and absolutely loved it. The private "couples only" glamping tents cost more than the rest of the glamping village, but for your own section of the beach and to be able to watch the sun rise and set over the waves; it's worth the cost.

Travel Like a Local

The Ritz Carlton at Elizabeth Quays.

When you want the height of bougee places to stay, you'll head here. Maybe

Just for ONE night because the price is borderline *obscene*.

Conveniently located at Elizabeth Quay, The Ritz-Carlton is an easy 5 minutes' walk from The Barrack Street Jetty or a 15-minute walk from the city's main malls. This 5-star hotel is made up of a gorgeous pool, 205 individually decorated guestrooms (featuring minibars and espresso maker) with complimentary Wifi.

Guests at the Ritz Carlton can chill out at the full-service spa while enjoying massages, body treatments, and facials. The Ritz Carlton also has an amazing outdoor pool, a sauna, and a 24-hour gym – although why anyone would want to be doing a workout while on holiday at such an amazing place is beyond me, but ok. Guests can get a fancy bite to eat at the Ritz's "Hearth Restaurant" or maybe unwind at the end of the day with a drink in the Lounge area or the poolside bar. Guests can get a cooked-to-order breakfast on weekdays from 7:00 AM to 10:00 AM for an extra fee.

The views alone across the whole of Elizabeth Quays jetty and waterways are worth the high prices for overnight stays in the beautifully appointed rooms.

The Pan Pacific

Perth's Pan Pacific is a short bus trip (or a long walk) from the heart of the city. It's more towards East Perth than the CBD but buses along the terrace will take you for free, and a new IGA about 10 minute's walk from the Pan Pacific is helpful for drinks and snacks you don't have to pay a fortune for if you use your hotel room's mini bar.

Guests can get comfy in one of the 486 air-conditioned rooms featuring LCD TV's, complimentary WIFI and cable programming for awesome movie nights. While you're staying at the Pan Pacific, make sure to take advantage of recreational opportunities offered, including an outdoor pool, a steam room, and a 24-hour fitness centre. Additional amenities at this hotel include complimentary wireless Internet access, concierge services, and babysitting (surcharge).

Grab a bite to eat at *Lobby Cafe*, one of the hotel's 2 restaurants, or stay in and take advantage of the 24-hour room service. Snacks are also available at the 2 coffee shops/cafes. If you need to unwind, you can take a break with a tasty beverage at one of the 2 bars/lounges. Buffet breakfasts are available daily from 6:00 AM to 11:00 AM for an additional fee. You can try to include a daily breakfast with you room booking online to make things tastier – I mean, easier. Lol. The menu looks amazing.

The Duxton

My husband Alun won a Duxton Gift Voucher on a University competition so off we went and omg we had so much fun. The rooms are really large and fancy, the pool area is gorgeous and the Duxton is really close to the Cathedral, Perth's Concert Hall and the Christmas lights trail if you stay during December. The beds are huge, and the linen is super soft. We had a great sleep and because we booked for our wedding anniversary, thoughtful Hotel staff had a complimentary bottle of wine and wine glasses out for us when we checked into the room. It's a beautiful hotel to spend a romantic night together as you can go for a walk in the evening to check out Perth's pretty light shows and then stroll back at your leisure and enjoy the beauty and space of your room.

AN ENTIRE BEACH PENTHOUSE – "BLU PETER" IN COOGEE.

What's better than staying by the Beach all summer? Staying in a freaking PENTHOUSE APARTMENT by the beach, that's what. If you have the bankroll, I highly recommend renting this gorgeous sea-side Penthouse and enjoying *an incredible weekend* by the sea at Coogee Beach. The views alone are breathtaking! Check these out:

Images sourced from AirBnB Perth (2023).

Travel Like a Local

This incredible Penthouse can be rented per night from the "AirBnB Perth" website at:

https://www.airbnb.com.au/rooms/28260359?source_impression_id=p3_1706951090_QFvxIyoHym4e08oM

This *absolutely amazing Penthouse* offers 360degree views of the stunning turquoise waters of Coogee Beach. You and your loved ones/or mates can access the gorgeous, pristine shore of Coogee Beach on your doorstep.

Styled by Blu Peter Homestore,
this apartment is tastefully decorated and is great for a couples getaway or for that special occasion. You have full private access to your own deck with BBQ, lounge area,
hammock and a large private spa. So sit back, put your feet up and relax while you watch the boats sail past.

A LESSER-KNOWN LUXURY "THE COMO HOTEL"

Set in stunning buildings that have kept their mid-19th Century fittings, COMO The Treasury is located in the heart of Perth's CBD. *COMO The Treasury* is really easy to get to – only a 15-minute walk from Perth Convention and Exhibition Centre and just a 2-minute walk from the main shops and restaurants of Hay Street Mall. Perth Airport is only a 20-minute drive away. Their rooms are beautifully decorated in earthy, relaxing tones of cream and beige, with modern styling.

Your *complimentary* (so fill your boots because it's **free**! Awesome!) mini bar is restocked daily. Other features include a flat-screen TV and a luxurious bathroom with bath robes, slippers and free toiletries. "*Post*" restaurant offers contemporary Italian cuisine, guided by the season's bounty and the best Western Australian produce available. The other onsite place to eat "*Wildflower*," is a stunning rooftop restaurant featuring views across the Swan River, serves contemporary cuisines boasting Western Australian produce. Other facilities on offer include a bougee concierge, valet parking and a helpful tour desk. You can enjoy a workout in the kitted out fitness centre, or pamper yourself at the Shambhala Spa offering facials and massages. Couples particularly like the location so it's suited for an amazing romantic getaway. A review from Booking.Com (sourced in Feb 2024) reads: *"Everything was wonderful - attentive but discreet staff, exceptionally comfortable and spacious room with beautiful bathroom, lovely pool upstairs and fantastic restaurants on site. We couldn't have wished for more."*

13. "YEAH, I CAN SPEND A BIT" PLACES TO STAY

Travelling is a little more challenging if you're counting every dollar. Before I tell you about some of Perth's most affordable places to lay your head, I thought we'd check out the 'in between' places which are all really beautiful and in great locations *but won't cost you a fortune* – especially if you're thinking of staying a week or more.

There are so many places I'm going to recommend and so much more I need to tell you about a holiday in Perth, so I'll just list the 20 best 'mid-range' Hotels to stay at and leave the detailed explanations on most of these for you to explore in your own time.

IBIS STYLES, East Perth is a *great* hotel to stay at when you're wanting something nice but not too expensive (Author's photo included). The rooms are really funky, bright and clean. The Ibis is in East Perth but a quick bus up the Terrace (if you tell the Driver you're just going into the city he will let you ride FOR FREE) will get you into the city and closer to Perth's main attractions. I've stayed here for some much needed "me time" and loved the youthful ambience as well as my crisp, clean room. It was great to grab breakfast in the Ibis Styles café then head out for the day.

QUEST – Kings Park or Mounts Bay Road – closer to the city

Art Series – the Adnate – the entire building looks and feels like a piece of artwork.

Oaks Perth Hotel (CBD)

Rydges Perth – Kings Square

East Perth Suites Hotel

The Westin, Perth.

Hyatt Regency. First of all, the breakfast buffet here (usually included in the price of room hire) is hands down one of the *best* in the world. I've never seen anything like it; the choices of sweet and savoury foods are endless. Everything is cooked to perfection and everything looks so good. All the food offered is the most delicious you can ever think of and it's well worth the price; you'll leave there so full you think you could pop, seriously. The Hyatt Regency host Conferences, Weddings, Business events and also put on one of the best high tea packages I've ever seen. I booked these guys for my Hen's night "high tea", and we were all so full by the end of that evening, with so many cute little desserts to choose from, an ice-cream bar and a menu of all the tea flavours you could imagine. Having a wide range of sweet and savoury canapes served kept us all happy and catered to each of our individual tastes. I highly recommend any meal here at the Hyatt, especially the high tea; it's worth the cost per head.

The Sebel – West Perth

"QT" – this hotel costs more than a lot of the others but is in the heart of the city so it's super convenient and worth the investment. The décor is very dark and not to my personal taste, but '*the in-room bathtubs are divine*' according to my friend Peta who had a recent staycation at the QT and she loved the dark colours in her room and throughout the hotel.

Tribe Hotel – Perth CBD

Doubletree by Hilton – Northbridge

Mercure Perth on Hay

Riverview on Mount Street

Quality Hotel Ambassador, Perth

Novotel Perth CBD – pricier side of hotels but nice

"THE ALEX HOTEL", Northbridge.

I'll stop here with listing and tell you a bit more about this hotel, because Perth's gorgeous, boutique "Alex" is worth writing about. Hotel Alex is probably the most beautiful little-known hotel in the whole of Perth. I only discovered it when my friend said we should try a cup of tea in their beautiful, bespoke café. I've walked past it so many times when I've travelled between the city centre and Northbridge but have wanted so many times to go in and see what it's like. When G and I were there for lunch, he asked a waitress if we could pop up and look at the rooms and she was lovely and showed one to us – it looked cosy and sweet. What caught my eye was the table with morning tea laid out for all guests – cupcakes, tea cakes, little sandwiches and pots of different tea. *That's* what I'd like to have waiting for me if I stayed in a hotel – so good! When G and I went back downstairs to finish our tea, I was *super stoked* to see an Australian celebrity was staying at the Alex! I tried to take a sneaky photo of The Living Room host Miguel, but he caught me, smiled and said "Come on over, you don't have to hide your camera" and put a friendly arm around me as G snapped a picture of us both. I was so excited and it was so nice to see that Miguel is a nice person in real life and not just on camera.

Luxury Hotel World's (2023) website calls the Alex Hotel "a hotel created to provide the inquisitive traveller homely comforts within the most vibrant of Perth's neighbourhoods. Within Alex's walls you will discover a dedication to delicious food, interesting wines, craft beers, artisan spirits, good reads, and the smell of great locally roasted coffee."

Thoughtfully designed, inviting common areas give plenty of opportunity to relax or catch up on work, while the beautifully crafted bedrooms provide sometimes much-needed quiet sanctuary from the surrounding Northbridge nightlife. Perth's city centre is less than a 5 minutes' walk away and the excitement of Perth's cultural precinct is on your doorstep.

The bedrooms at Alex range from cosy and intimate to those with a little more space. Importantly, they all come complete with super comfortable beds, hand crafted furniture, the latest smart TV's, free Wi-Fi and much welcomed fresh air from opening windows or private balconies. Guests can enjoy a drink and relax on the rooftop terrace, which offers beautiful views of the city. *Alex Hotel Perth* is a short 10-minute walk from Hay Street Shopping Area and a quick 10-minute drive from Kings Park and Botanic Garden for some great sightseeing. Perth Airport is a 20-minute drive away.

Crowne Plaza Perth CBD – close to Elizabeth Quay
Holiday Inn, City Centre
Mantra – on Hay

Travel Like a Local

REALLY COOL LOW BUDGET PLACES TO STAY – PARTICULARLY IF YOU'RE A BACKPACKER

14. AFFORDABLE PLACES - KANGAROO INN

Situated right in the heart of the city, *Kangaroo Inn* is one of the most affordable places to stay if you're travelling on a tight budget and don't mind a "no frills" place to hang out. With an impressive decked communal area, neat and tidy private or shared rooms (rooms with bunk beds) and amenities for guests including a massive pool table, spacious dining area for guest to eat together, and an open, inviting lobby for the weary backpackers of this world. The online photos look really nice and Kangaroo Inn looks like a fairly decent place to stay.

15. AFFORDABLE PLACES – SPINNERS BACKPACKERS (NORTHBRIDGE)

I've checked out the cool, funky-fresh website and **Spinners looks like the place to be when you're on a tight budget and don't mind sharing a room**. Out of all the backpackers places I've seen, *this hostel is the one I'd stay at if push came to shove because it's newly built, beautifully decorated and I like the clean, clear, bright outdoor areas*. The team at Spinners claim: "Chilled vibe is still here, *but everything else is new*. Like the new design led bedrooms, bathrooms, courtyards and kitchen. Oh, did we mention the really, really fast free internet? EVERYTHING ABOUT OUR CONCEPT IS GENEROUS; from the commercial sized kitchen to the king single beds." Spinners boasts about their built-in pretty outdoor BBQ space, a large (newly built, so there's that) shared kitchen and eye-catching vertical gardens. Spinners provide individual computer nooks by each bed to the XL personal lockers for each guest. Spinners is the start of a new generation of backpackers. If you're staying at Spinners, you can book a Private "Ooh La Lah" room with one single and one double bed – perfect for the couple where someone involved always wants to bring their bestie along, I guess? LOL. Or you can rent out a "mixed" or "king single" dorm where 6-8 beds will be in one large room. Spinners also offer "female only" rooms for girls who feel more comfortable sharing with other girls instead of mixed bunks.

16. AFFORDABLE PLACES – BEATTY LODGE (LEEDERVILLE)

This is the only lodge I've actually stayed in – twice - so I can tell you about this place from experience. Beatty Lodge is a very 'no frills' place but it's clean, tidy and all the staff are really cool. They've had a revamp since I last stayed and have different types of rooms to rent. It all looks more modern and still has the cool student vibe it always prides itself on. The Beatty Lodge website (2023) says *"Centrally located just 3km (10 mins via bus) from Perth city, Beatty Lodge is ideal for students. Stay a week, a semester or even a year with our range of budget conscious rooms that are available for short and long-term stays. With over 20+ nationalities under one roof, you will feel right at home in our multicultural student residence."*

Beatty Lodge is the only hostel that has a pool. It's also pretty easy to get to. You can either catch one of the many buses into the city along the main road Beatty is set by, or you can go on a short walk to the Leederville train station.

There is a wide choice of private rooms (my recommendation), shared twin rooms, 4 and 6 person dorms as well as a spacious self-serve kitchen equipped with cooking appliances (not all things are included in kitchen use though – have your own tongs, spatulas and things to *make* meals with, so you're not at a total loss like Gracie and I were in when we tried to make spaghetti there one night), fridges and ovens enabling you to save money and be independent. There are shared, gendered bathrooms and showers on every floor ensuring you are never far from essential amenities. I recommend wearing thongs in the bathrooms and during your shower just to keep your feet free from any weird infections. Beatty Lodge offers shared rooms which are always allocated by gender, ensuring privacy and comfort for all residents.

17. AFFORDABLE PLACES – DOWNTOWN BACKPACKERS HOSTEL

Again, I'm surprised how nice this place looks when I checked out their cool website. Location: 57-59 Bennett Street East Perth 6004. This hostel is located in Perth City Eastern End about 10 minutes' walk down Hay Street to the CBD. The team at Downtown Backpackers require a passport for booking and aim to 'create a home away from home' while you stay with them. The Downtown team provide shared kitchen facilities, Netflix, quiet gathering areas and spacious safe rooms. If you stay here, you can opt for a private room or a shared bunk in one of their dormitories. Building Community is key here and the staff and guests often go to the bar together Wednesday and Thursdays in nearby Northbridge with some FREE beer included.

18. AFFORDABLE PLACES – SPRIALS BACKPACKERS (NORTHBRIDGE)

With a 4.7 star rating out of 5 stars, this hostel might be a contender for a great place to stay with a funky community vibe and comfortable shared spaces to get to know the other guests. The Spiral website states: "*At Spiral, we aim to provide a clean and safe environment whilst creating a meeting place for like-minded travellers in a fun and chilled atmosphere. We hope that our love of travel and variety of experiences have helped create a place where you can make new friends and feel comfortable for however long you stay with us. We are located in the heart of Northbridge, Perth's main entertainment district with its uncountable bars, clubs, restaurants, museums and art galleries such as the Art Gallery of WA and the Perth Convention and Exhibition*

Centre. We have good sized dorm rooms. Each room has centrally controlled air conditioning, is well ventilated and has a skylight. **Due to the design of the building the rooms do not have windows.**"

No windows. Huh. **That might be something to note depending on how claustrophobic you are.**

Conveniently based inside Perth's *Free Transit Zone*, you can catch the Blue CAT bus to the Hostel's front door which is pretty cool. The Hostel is only a 10-minute walk to Perth railway station and Perth's main Bus port. Spirals is proud to be "*on the doorstep of Perth's CBD where you can find endless shops and malls and a stone's throw from central attractions such as Elizabeth Quay and King's Park Botanical Garden.*"

The team at Spiral offer rooms all with bunk beds, they provide bed linen (as they bloody should, honestly!) and towels are available on request. All rooms have air conditioning. The Lodge has a large kitchen with walk in fridge. Washing machines and dryers are available. In addition to the kitchen and communal areas, Spirals also offers free WIFI, free PlayStation Wii, a free foosball/soccer table, free table tennis and free Netflix – so that's cool. The staff also have free drinks vouchers for several of the best bars and clubs in town.

Travel Like a Local

19. PERTH'S MOST POSH PLACES TO EAT

These guys are the *top 5* when it comes to fine dining here in Perth:

Fine dining at the C Restaurant (Level 33, 44 St Georges Terrace) – **for 360-degree views in a *rotating* restaurant.** Yep, you heard right – as you dine, the restaurant slowly spins around; letting you see mind-blowing views across the entire city of Perth. A whole rotation takes about 90 minutes, so it gives you time to savour every bite of your gourmet meal as you see something new every time you look up from your plate. This is *the* place for fine dining and *even better views*. I recommend going just before sunset, it's incredible. My husband and I have been to the C Restaurant for each of our birthdays and took each of our Mom's on Mother's day. I've also taken my bestie for high tea on her visit from England (I wanted to show off, we had so much fun) and were able to afford these by downloading a voucher from Groupon. They have regular deals for the C Restaurant on their site, so whenever you're travelling to Perth, download a specials voucher and experience the C restaurant without having to spend everything you saved in one night. Be warned - because the restaurant rotates - when you get up to go to the toilet, you'll come out and be at an entirely different section of the dining area. Don't panic, just ask a helpful staff member to guide you back to your table – they're used to it. Also don't put your handbag down on the outer rim of the restaurant, it *will* travel around the dining area without you.

Fine Dining at Nobu (part of the Crown Casino):

Now, I haven't tried dining here as high-end Japanese food isn't my jam (I love me a kebab, ok?) but my mates have been to Nobu. My foodie-obsessed friend Sarita said *the food was beyond delicious* and highly recommends going there for a night out. **Nobu is the world's most recognised Japanese restaurant** and is known for its innovative new style Japanese cuisine. Esteemed Chef Nobu Matsuhisa brings his reputable fusion of traditional Japanese cuisine with South American flavours to create the unique dining experience that is Nobu. Experience famed signature dishes that Nobu is known and loved for all around the world. Including the Black Cod Miso and Yellowtail Sashimi with Jalapeño, these along with a selection from Chef de Cuisine Pingping Poh's own innovative creations form Nobu Perth's exquisite must-try menu. Complemented by an extensive menu of refreshing cocktails, sake, premium spirits, a range of beer and world-class wines. **Definitely book ahead** and reserve a table if you plan to try Nobu out as it's popular and not somewhere you can just turn up and eat – unlike the Kebab place around the corner from my house. *So good.*

Fine Dining at Wildflower (part of 'Como the Treasury' Hotel):

Occupying the stunning rooftop space of COMO The Treasury (they have an incredible view from floor-to-ceiling windows), Wildflower serves lunch and dinner against a backdrop of sweeping views across the Swan River and city of Perth. **Wildflower's fine dining contemporary dishes revolve around the indigenous ethos of "6 seasons"** with farmer and forager-driven menus. The menu changes regularly to reflect which of the 6 seasons are at the forefront when you dine and allows guests to experience fine dining that embraces honouring Indigenous peoples and culture. The incredible staff at Wildflower proudly boast: *"Native ingredients play an integral role in our story and menus. Our produce and ingredients are sourced from suppliers with a respect for this land."* You can learn more about the Noongar 6 seasons here: https://wildflowerperth.com.au/noongar-six-seasons/

Fine Dining at 'FyRE' (located at Connolly Shopping Centre):

Vegans. Not my people. I am a proud carnivore and as such, I LOVE that FyRE's motto is "no vegans" - so good. If you've got the dollars, pop in and discover the remarkable meaty world of FyRE; an extraordinary restaurant nestled in the heart of Perth's "Pom world" (legit, there are sooo many English people here in Perth), Connolly. Led by the talented Chef Johnnie Mountain, FyRE has gained a reputation for its exceptional cuisine and unforgettable dining experiences. We haven't tried it (yet) but Alun and I want to go on a Sunday and try out FyRE's "MAD Sunday Roast" – complete with Yorkshire puddings. An eclectic bunch of locals and expats lead by renown Chef Johnnie Mountain, the team at FyRE aims to create unforgettable experiences for our patrons. One of the reviewers for FyRE rates the restaurant as *"Absolutely f**king chaotic"*. I don't know why, but I feel drawn in by that. I love me a little chaos during dinner. It would feel like being at home. There are quite a few angry reviews by disgruntled Vegans on the FyRE website and again, that makes me want to go even more.

Fine dining at Rockpool Bar & Grill (located at the Crown Casino) – this Restaurant serves an *insane* "Rare Breed Steak Tasting Dinner" (just a head's up - it's

really, really expensive to order) with steak tartare en Croute canape's paired with Italian Sour No. 3. The entrée is baby cos salad with buttermilk dressing, leading into the main which is made up of 5 different cuts of steak served with potato and cabbage gratin. You'll finish off with a dessert of Catherine's passionfruit pavlova. Alternatively, if you don't want to have to re-mortgage your house for a night's fine dining, you can order Rockpool's signature burger and chips plus draught beer for a tenth of the price. Just quietly, I know which option I'll be going with next time Alun and I have a free date night.

20. SMASH A MEAL WITH THE LOCALS

The Woodbridge Hotel in Guildford easily has the best in-house 'tasting plate' in the whole of Australia. The Woodbridge crew go all out in giving you a delicious sample of chicken, curry of the day (Eg Pork Vindaloo served with rice, paratha and poppadum's), fish (the fish of the day will be printed on the blackboard) and chips, bruschetta, slices of chorizo, the soup of the day *and* house-made sausage rolls. To date, I've not heard of so much variety with so many different meals offered in the one share plate from any other establishment, so definitely stop in and give this a go.

Toastface GRILLAH – Perth's *best* toasted sandwiches ever. My friends and I used to get these gourmet toasties at their 'hole in the wall' café next to Woolies in the city, but they branched out with 2 other stores and closed their city café. Nowadays, you can get these herb-filled, golden, crunchy, delicious, toasted sandwiches at their new locations in Northbridge or at Scarborough Beach. You can also order these bad boys for delivery using your UberEats ap. I highly recommend these gourmet bites to eat; the Toastface crew take toasted sandwich experience to the next level.

The Beaufort Street Food Markets – Monday evenings during summer. These markets are such a great way to get to hang out with Perth locals and get to know them. On a Monday evening, most of Beaufort Street (one of our busiest and main streets to the city from our Northern suburbs) lights right up. Food trucks from so many different provinces line up and on one evening, you get a huge choice of food from Asian, Mexican, Korean, French, Aussie, UK and European sellers. Maybe some African food, too. My husband and I love grabbing a tasty bao bun for dinner and I'll always stop at the food van that makes these tiny, fluffy miniature pancakes and coats them in maple syrup with banana – or whatever the other delicious choices are. They're amazing and my favourite dessert. The markets start at around 950 (ish) Beaufort street, so come early, park up and grab something tasty for dinner.

Alfred's kitchen (in Guildford). OMG What an absolute *classic*. When you go to Alfred's, you're going to one of Perth's most incredible local places to 'grab a feed'. Alfred's was established eons ago. It started out as just one tiny food tent and a fireplace. It's grown now to have a main structure for cooking meals, proper seating and even a tram to check out, but the fireplace is still there and on a cool Autumn or Spring night, it's incredible to sit on logs around the fireplace with complete strangers but feel like you're all a family, somehow as you smile at each other over tomato-sauce smiles and the best burgers and hotdogs you'll ever get your hands on. My brother said Alfred's is the only place in the world where you'll see a rich CEO *and a homeless guy* sit on the *same* log at the *same campfire* and talk like equals, and that's pretty amazing. There's something incredibly special about Alfred's kitchen and I highly recommend going. Go for the amazing experience of sharing a meal together as one happy bunch, but stay for the awesome wood-fired taste of the hotdogs and burgers they serve. They taste of community. Of togetherness.

Smash a meal in the sunshine at the Rose and Crown – This gorgeous pub is a truly impressive Western Australian landmark. The stately Rose & Crown is set on 2.5 acres of gorgeous Aussie bushland and commands a prominent position amongst the variety of shops and cafés gracing leafy Swan Street in Guildford. This historic hotel; built way back in 1841 and located at the gateway to the state's beautiful Swan Valley region, has provided a welcome resting place for travellers and visitors. Registered with the National Trust, the Rose & Crown has stood the test of time and today is a popular attraction among locals and tourists. Link:

https://www.rosecrown.com.au/ Because it's such a historic place, my husband loves "going to the spooky bar" which used to be old tunnels beneath the Rose and Crown's foundation. The underground section is a lot cooler than above and still has some of its original old barrels. The tunnels are closed for safety but it's still fun to go down the ladder and into the unknown.

Grab a Curry at East Perth IGA: These curries are the *bomb*, seriously. The IGA on Royal Street in East Perth is small, but packs a punch when it comes to grabbing a quick lunch. They serve either options for a roast beef meal with baked vegetables or for one of the best curries you're likely to have. Their curry selection is small – they have about 6 different types on offer – but each type is really delicious and comes with a selection of boiled or saffron rice, vegetables and fluffy naan bread. So good.

Treat yourself to the best fish and chips ever from "Sweetlips Fish and Chips" Another great way to eat local without breaking the bank; *Sweetlips* serves *fantastic* fish and chips in Leederville, Fremantle and Scarborough. Something about the way they cook and season their fish and chips is next level. The fish is always crisp on the outside and 'meaty' on the inside. All the chips are golden, delicious and have just the right amount of sea salt. Having

this familiar meal with your mates is a great way to spend an evening. All of the seafood used by "SweetLips" is sourced local from within WA; with fish from Shark Bay Whiting to Cone Bay Barramundi. Their produce is fresh from the ocean - never from the freezer. Michael Waldock (Sweetlips Managing Director) embraces using local produce to support WA's economy. Michael states: *"In a global economy where imported food products can be stored for weeks and months before reaching the dinner table, local WA produce provides an opportunity to eat food that is caught, picked and harvested recently, then eaten and enjoyed immediately – as food is supposed to be. Sweetlips' range of WA fish fillets and other local produce provides this opportunity for customers to enjoy this fresh food experience while supporting the WA economy."*
Website: sweetlips.com.au

TALK TO ME ABOUT Donuts. All the best

donuts can be found on Beaufort Street, Mt Lawley. You can either pop into *Mary St Bakery* (they have a 'special donut' for every week), '*Chubby Boy*' with amazing Asian-inspired donuts and desserts or the *IGA in Mt Lawley* who also offer a great selection of delicious donuts.

Travel Like a Local

Authentic Bites Dumpling House – Located in Northbridge – (*whenever I walk by, there's always a long line outside, which is a bloody good sign, isn't it?*). Founded in 2016, this amazing restaurant was created out of a genuine love for dumplings, and it shows in every dish they serve. The Authentic Bites menu features a wide variety of dumplings, including pork, chicken and prawn, and vegetable options. Each dumpling is carefully crafted with the freshest ingredients and traditional techniques, ensuring that every bite is bursting with flavour. But dumplings aren't the only thing on the menu at Authentic Bites, the team also offer a range of other dishes such as noodle soups, rice bowls, and appetizers like squid tentacles and crispy chicken bites. Whether you're in the mood for a quick lunch or a leisurely dinner, Authentic Bites Dumpling House is the perfect spot to satisfy your dumpling craving.

And get this, you guys – **Authentic Bites have a robot servant in Northbridge and three of them in Karrinyup** that can serve you dishes for an enjoyable dining experience! I mean WHAT?!? A robot servant! So cool. It's worth going in to visit just for the robots!

The team at Authentic Bites strive to bring only the best Shanghai Xiao Long Bao, Wontons and other gorgeous little dumplings to Perth's thriving food culture. Everyone at Authentic Bites works hard to deliver authentic Chinese flavours, fresh ingredients, and top quality hand-made dumplings cooked to order.

Scarborough Beach Night Markets – Smashing a meal with some friendly locals on one of the prettiest coastlines you'll ever see – even at night. Every Thursday evening from 2nd November through to the end of April, the Scarborough Beach markets are on and they are amazing. Food trucks serving food from all over the world line up at the Beach's main entrance. You can combine a great feed with the sights and sounds of Scarborough just as the sun goes down. The vendors do great meals of fish and chips, pies, hotdogs, Asian food, Mexican tacos – the list goes on and on. The vendors change often, so hop onto the Scarborough Beach Night Markets website to find a list of vendors that will be setting up that week: https://scarboroughsunsetmarkets.com/this-weeks-vendors this Thursday, for instance (tonight. I might swing by and check them out myself, it's been a while) one of the vendors specializes in fairy floss (OMG my favourite!) while others will be serving Gnocchi, beef jerky, Thai and Mexican food – along with "not guilty" ice cream. So good.

Travel Like a Local

21. TRAVELLING SOLO

This section is written for the introvert or lone traveller (my personal preference – I like seeing things in my own time at my own pace) who enjoys their own company and wants to check things out by themselves. *I see you*. Here are the best spots to check out – on your own:

Solo Traveller – The Perth Mint – As well as getting to learn all about Perth's goldmining history, you get to see a guy pour melted gold into a bar shape, it's really cool. You can also get your own customised coin with a short message of your choosing printed on it. My husband has 3 of these and loves them. He also made one for his parents who were here visiting from Wales and another for one of his best friends as a leaving gift before Troy went on a massive road trip all throughout Australia. The personalised coins look beautiful, are sturdy so they last and make great gifts for someone you're thinking of while on your solo tour.

Solo amongst the books at Perth City Library (Hay Street) – this recently built place of wonder and books is my 'go to' when I want somewhere cool and quiet to hang out. The books are all amazing and range from contemporary romances to historical books and maps. The floor-to-ceiling windows in so many sections of the library are gorgeous and there are so many places to study, browse the net or just enjoy the silence and feel of a proper book (none of this 'kindle' nonsense).

A Tour for One at Perth's Museum – You can wander about for a donation of just a few gold coins and go and see the 'open to public' exhibits, or you can pay a little more and go to a guided tour and see way more exhibits and themed sections of the museum. The museum is vast and filled with so many things to see and learn about. It's an amazing place to stroll about at your leisure and learn about history in your own time.

Solo time to admire the Perth Art Gallery – As someone who knows nothing about the fundamentals of art, *I love this place*. I haven't studied art history and don't know what makes art so amazing, but I know what I like and *don't like* when it comes to paintings, drawings, sculptures and even some of the free talks and shows they have available - and going to the Art gallery is a great way to remind myself of that. I love walking around and taking all the beautiful paintings and sculptures in. I even have my two favourite paintings – one of a maiden on a horse with a knight in shining armour riding next to her and keeping her safe. The expression on her face gives me the feeling she's capable of protecting herself and I like that. The other painting is called "The Bushman" and is a man sitting in the Aussie outback at dusk, poking a fire. I like that the artist captured the muted colours and tones of 'dusk' so beautifully. Whenever I look at the painting, I can almost smell the gumtrees and the fire. Something about it is so natural and so Australian. I love seeing it.

A 'Walking Tour' for one, Please – Perth CBD and Kings Park. My friend Cat was visiting from Liverpool UK and did a solo walking tour with an Indigenous Aboriginal guide around Kings Park. She learnt so many interesting things about the history of Kings Park from an Aboriginal person's point of view which is incredibly important and probably the best way to learn about Perth's origins. My friend Amy took the "inner city" walking tour and was amazed at the really cool 'secret' places the tour guide showed her. Amy said it was well worth it and was excited to know about hidden bars and special rooftop gardens she would have never known about otherwise.

Take yourself on a super fancy **Solo Movie Date** at *Palace Cinemas Platinum Club* – Raine Square, Perth City Centre. This is hands down my favourite thing to do. "Me time" is my favourite way to refill my 'self-love' cup and Palace Cinemas are the most beautiful place in the whole of Perth (in my opinion – I like luxury ok?) to see the latest blockbuster. The Platinum Club option for the movies is the limousine of movies. It's the GOLD CLASS standard and it is absolutely AMAZING. It's worth paying a little extra for large, leather, fully-reclinable seats and a menu with Perth's best wines, craft beers and wonderful meals that make your movie experience feel like you've won the lottery. Palace Cinemas are beautiful whether you go lux or to the 'normal' theatres. They do amazing "olive oil" popcorn with sea-salt and their bougee version of 'choc-tops' are next level. Because it's a fairly new cinema complex, the seats, carpet, drapes and toilets are all new and I love that.

22. ROMANTIC COUPLES ACTIVITIES TO DO

For me, it's the best thing ever to have a better half (I'm low-key obsessed with my husband) so I wanted to list the most fun things to do as a couple when you're on holidays here in Perth.

On a clear and balmy night, you could start out with Perth's Outdoor Movies – these are held on a Car Park rooftop (shh! This is a local's secret) **'Rooftop Movies'** is located in the heart of Northbridge, surrounded by the hustle and bustle of Perth's most thriving entertainment precinct. You can find us on Level 6 of the CPP Roe Street Car Park. The producers of "Fringe World Festival" (this awesome festival runs every year) present an open-air cinema experience like no other. Serving sunset drinks, awesome foods on their ever-changing menu and movies under the stars - atop a rooftop carpark with panoramic city views all summer long. It honestly feels awesome getting into the lift with people just collecting their cars and knowing you're on your way to a movie. It's like a secret little club to belong to, with movies, popcorn and amazing views. Click onto the "Rooftop Movies" website to find out what's showing and buy tickets here: https://rooftopmovies.com.au/ . The Rooftop movies run from the end of October onwards until the end of April.

Dates with Romantic Candlelit music – highly recommend going to the COLDPLAY one – we went to the Beatles tribute, too – but it wasn't as good. "Candlelight" by FEVER provides the most amazing musical experience with tributes to popular artists reimagined by a small orchestral group. Link to buy tickets and see what upcoming shows there are: https://feverup.com/en/perth/candlelight Fever have added new tributes to Taylor Swift and Ed Sheeran which is really cool.

Romantic Picnics in the Park – For a romantic picnic, you could go to the Claisebrook Inlet and pick a grassy knoll with an amazing view across the river. When my husband and I were first dating, we'd bring big bits of cardboard and slide down the hill. You can also picnic with the one you love outside the Optus Stadium; especially if someone's holding a concert and you can sit and listen for free. My husband and I had a picnic outside Optus Stadium when ColdPlay were here, and we had the best time. So many other couples, mates and families had the same idea and we all sat together in common poorness (Ha! The tix were so expensive, right?) and sing along to the greatest hits. Packing some sandwiches or wraps, some drinks and a picnic blanket is all you'll need for that romantic experience.

Hang out with your other half at Kings Park. Kings Park is one of the world's largest and most beautiful inner-city parks, and it sits in our backyard. It's a place of rich cultural heritage and indigenous significance, drawing almost six million visitors a year.

With over 3,000 of Western Australia's native plant species thriving there, Kings Park really is Mother Nature's art gallery. However, the plants are not the only work of art you'll find - Kings Park is the number one destination for those wanting to take in the magnificence of the Perth city skyline. Whether it's the orange hues of the sunset reflecting against the glass panels of the skyscrapers or the lights that glisten and twinkle at night, the view truly feels unreal every time. Immerse yourself in the beauty of the Western Australian Botanic Garden and embark on a journey of discovery as you learn about the state's diverse flora. With more than nine gardens displaying everything from trees and shrubs to wildflowers, you'll be in awe as you come across rare and stunning plant species sourced from the all around WA's Great Southern all the way up to the Northern Kimberley.

Experience the best of what Kings Park has to offer as you wander beside banksia trees that gently sway in the breeze and walk beneath the serenading sounds of kookaburra laughs. Discover the vibrant botanic gardens and be captivated by local artworks and surrounding views; amongst this, indulge in nourishing culinary delights, ultimately soaking up all that this Perth hotspot has to offer.

These more exciting options are available for a fun-filled date, too:

- **Escape Rooms** – Northbridge or in the Perth's city centre.
- **Matagarup Bridge Zip Line** (over 300 steps to climb – make sure you're able to cope)
- **Axe Throwing**
- **Bowling in the CBD**
- **Fremantle Markets**
- e-Scooting around Mandurah to see **THE MANDURAH GIANTS**

23. FAMILY FRIENDLY ACTIVITIES – SCITECH

For all the little scientists, *this* is the place to be. It's a science-based museum where unlike other museums - you can touch and play with *everything*. Nothing is off limits. Even the grown-ups love it.

As a not-for-profit organisation, for more than three decades Scitech has brought engaging and entertaining science experiences to everyone from adventure-ready kids to inquisitive adults – igniting a lifelong curiosity in the process. The Scitech team believe in experiences that engage the hands will also engage the mind – whether you're three or 103, it's hard not to learn when you're exploring and asking questions.

At the *Scitech Discovery Centre* in West Perth, their interactive exhibits, Chevron Science Theatre, Puppet Theatre live shows, excursion programs, and events are designed, created, developed and built by our people in-house to get visitors talking about their experience long after they've left the centre. The Scitech planetarium is one of the largest in the Southern Hemisphere and allows visitors to be fully immersed as they explore the night sky and further into space.

Scitech's amazing digital offerings help us bring science experiences to an even wider audience including podcasts, Scitech's awesome YouTube series "Toy Tear Down" or "Science at Home" activities and 'Particle' - Scitech's independent media hub that connects young adults to science stories from Western Australia and beyond.

At the centre of everything Scitech does is how highly they value interpersonal relatinships. The crew at Scitech know that the biggest impact they can make is through the engaging and meaningful interactions visitors can have with Science Communicators and staff, so time to ask questions and learn from one-to-one conversations is infused throughout everything Scitech does.

The Team at Scitech (2023) are proud to announce: *"Our purpose is to inspire engagement by all Western Australians in science, technology, engineering and mathematics. At Scitech, we're here for anyone who has ever asked "why?" Because while answers are important, it's the questions that really get us thinking."*

24. TAKE THE FAMILY TO HILLARY'S HARBOR

Hillarys Boat Harbour (Located at 86 Southside Drive Hillarys) is only 25 minutes from the Perth CBD and is accessible by water, car, bus, foot, bicycle and *even helicopter.*

What we locals refer to as "Hillarys" has been developed to be as inclusive as possible; providing a variety of facilities to cater for people with disabilities, including a universal access floating pontoon, fishing platform, beach access pathway, a beach wheelchair, accessible barbeque facilities, drinking fountains and hotel rooms specifically tailored for people with limited mobility. My friends and I love going to Hillarys over the

Travel Like a Local

summer and hanging out around the boardwalk, listening to music, having an icecream or treating ourselves to a hearty pub meal and then going for a walk along the beach.

The Hillarys Boat Harbour has gone through a change in the last decade, having been burnt down in June 2003, then rebuilt to be stronger and more beautiful than before. It's our favourite place to hang out in the summer – eating delicious desserts, going to the sea-side pubs and watching little ones build sandcastles or paddle in the safe, calm inlet that makes Hillarys one of the best places to take a family. Hillaries has a range of shops to get the best bathers, boardshorts, dresses, handmade gifts or printed artworks.

25. TAKE THE FAMILY TO "AQWA" AQUARIUM

Check out one of the biggest ever aquariums where you can explore 12,000 km of Western Australia's underwater coastline in just a few hundred metres. From the icy waters of the southern ocean to the tropical wonderland of coral reefs in the Far North, AQWA takes you on an underwater journey to discover the amazing and resilient marine life of Western Australia.

Since 1988, AQWA has presented the beauty and wonder of this coastal environment and is Western Australia's main marine attraction. Keeping everything within a Western Australian theme, everything in AQWA can be found in the State's oceans. In addition, everything within Aqua displays is living – including the incredible complex marine environments and coral! When you go to Aqua, you get to see over 40 stunning exhibits; including one of the largest living coral reef exhibits in the world and Australia's largest aquarium displaying AQWA's shipwreck coast. It's also the 10th largest in the world!

In total, AQWA holds an incredible *4 million litres of water* and is home to over 4,000 fish. There's a special section where families can even interact with live sea animals at the touch pool. It's a great shallow pool for little ones to touch starfish, coral and seashells.

If you fancy it, I recommend getting tickets and going on AQWA's glass bottom boat tour. The glass bottom boat looks amazing and is something families would really like to experience together. The tour goes for about 30 minutes and you'll get to hear all about marine life from a knowledgeable Ocean Guide. Sessions available daily with a maximum of 9 participants per session.

26. FAMILY FRIENDLY ADVENTURE WORLD THEME PARK

Perth's best rides and slides are all at Adventure world. Bring the kids, bathers, sunscreen, hats and your courage to try out all the rides. Located at 351 Progress Drive, Bibra Lake – Adventure World is only 25 minutes' drive from Perth and only 15 minutes from Fremantle by car. The Theme Park is easily accessible by public transport (take the Mandurah Train Line to Cockburn Station then jump on the 520 bus (it runs every 30 mins on weekdays and every hour on weekends) to Fremantle which will drop you off at the entrance of Adventure World.

Adventure World is Perth's only Theme Park/ Water Park, set in beautifully landscaped botanical gardens and lawns with over 25 rides and attractions to enjoy, including the new world-class, exhilarating thrill ride *Goliath*; a giant pendulum swing ride. When I went with my family (I was much, much younger), they had a Pirate Ship ride which is much like the giant pendulum swing ride they have there now. I was 8 years old and as the pendulum got higher, I decided it wasn't for me and tried to climb out. Luckily Dad grabbed the back of my overalls and quick-thinking staff stopped the ride. So yeah, make sure your kids are definitely up for the 'scarier' rides and keep a careful eye on them the whole time. Adventure world features two heart thumping, adrenaline pumping roller-coasters – the *Abyss* and *Kraken* and bring your bathers and towels so you guys can try out the longest, tallest and steepest funnel water slide on the planet. Plus, there's the ever-popular Hawaiian resort themed Kahuna Falls, an Aussie Wildlife Experience and the enchanting Dragon's Kingdom for our younger adventurers to name just a few.

27. FAMILY FRIENDLY WATERSLIDES AT OUTBACK SPLASH

Located on the doorstep of the Swan Valley, just 30 minutes from the City, Perth's Outback Splash has long been one of WA's top outdoor entertainment destinations. Open September to April, in addition to thrilling waterslides and resort-style attractions, the Park includes mini golf, mazes, and sensory play activities.

In July 2006, local business owners Paul and Nicole Woodcock purchased The Maze with a vision to add new attractions and continue to build on the existing facilities.

The Splash Island waterslide playground, the Park's first water attraction, opened in December 2013 and the

Travel Like a Local

Octopus Bay Kids Splash Zone was opened in December 2016 to cater for the increasing 'young families' market.

In November 2019 the Park introduced four new and unique waterslides; these are regarded as the best of their kind in Australia and by far some of the most thrilling waterslide experiences in WA. The addition of the waterslide tower brings Perth's Outback Splash another step closer to its long term vision of being Perth's favourite water park destination, a must visit tourist attraction for all ages.

28. ROTTNEST "WADJEMUP" ISLAND

This. Is. What. You. Came. For.

"Rotto" as the locals call it – is one of the most beautiful islands you'll ever see in your life. Also called "Wadjemup" in honour of our First Nations People/Aboriginal people, this incredible island paradise is surrounded in clear turquoise waters. This island is also a haven for the cutest animals ever is somewhere you really need to see; the Quokkas.

Although the island meets the warm weather expectations of Perth, it also benefits from the cooling effect of the Indian Ocean breeze, so the temperatures always stay a few degrees below the city which is awesome when you need a break from the constant dry heat of summer.

On Wadjemup/Rottnest Island, the average temperatures during summer are:
December: 25.1°C – 17.7°C
January: 26.5°C – 19.1°C
February: 27.2°C – 19.5°C

Rottnest Island's website (2023) declares: "*Wadjemup, the Noongar name of the island, is often referred to as 'the place across the water where the spirits are'. This land is that of the Traditional Owners, the Whadjuk Noongar people, who know the island as a resting place of the spirits, as well as a memorial place of Aboriginal men and boys whose bodies still rest beneath the sands of Wadjemup. This is a history that we acknowledge and pay respect to.*"

Getting across to Rotto requires a boat. The best packages are from the 3 main ferry companies - *Rottnest Express*, *Sealink* or (you'll need to add a couple more bucks) hop on the *Rottnest Fast ferries* that leave from either Hillary's Boat Harbor, from the City (not recommended, it's the longest ferry ride and will definitely

Travel Like a Local

test your patience) or from Fremantle. If you're staying in the city's closely surrounding suburbs, you can catch a train into the city centre and then get on the Fremantle line to take you into the Fremantle Ports, ready to get the ferry over to the best adventure ever. Ferries depart from Northport (Rous Head) and B Shed (Victoria Quay) in Fremantle, Barrack Street Jetty in Perth's city centre and Hillarys Boat Harbour. When you're ready to head home, ferries depart from Main Jetty on the island in Thomson Bay at all different times throughout the day and into the early evening. On normal days, the last ferry is around 6:30pm but on special holidays, they extend ferry return hours until 9:00pm.

From finding a variety of stunning beaches and booking exquisite snorkelling tours, to planning rugged bush hikes (you can even rent out eBikes and do a lot less work as you cycle around Rotto) to walking around and learning historical stories that help you understand a different side to the island, Rotto is a gorgeous place to discover, explore, refresh, and reflect.

Things to do in Rottnest:

With more than 63 secluded beaches and 20 bays to choose from on Rottnest Island, you can choose your own adventure. Rotto is a haven for swimming, fishing, surfing, hiking and diving. Hop on and off the Island Explorer bus and do a hot lap of the island to find your patch of paradise.

Depending on what you feel like engaging in, you and your family can take a Rottnest Segway tour,

Cycle the Island (visit the salt flats, the lighthouses and a huge bloody cannon), Take the bus tour which stops at the main tourist lookouts/attractions on Rotto, go snorkelling in one of the many calm, beautiful bays, sit on the edge of the Basin and take in the sunshine, or grab a feed and a cold drink at the awesome sea-side pub in Thompson's Bay. Rottnest is also a great place to celebrate Australia day with live bands, family friendly activities, fireworks and a later ferry back to the city at 9pm.

Feel free to check out the main Rottnest site for a list of fun things to do on your Rotto holiday at:
https://www.rottnestisland.com/visit/guides-tips

Travel Like a Local

29. CITY OF PERTH ZOO

Lions and tigers and bears, Oh my!

Before you visit the zoo, I recommend hopping onto the Zoo's website and downloading the Zoo itinerary for the day you've chosen to visit so you'll know which shows to get to (and what times) for the best experience at the zoo from this link: https://perthzoo.wa.gov.au/suggested-itineraries. Also, bring sun cream with you, wear a hat and drink plenty of water – especially if you're visiting the Zoo during summer.

Perth's Zoo is probably one of the only attractions in Perth that's open every day of the year (including Christmas Day, Good Friday, Australia Day and New Year's Day) 9am to 5pm. The Zoo also opens for special evening events (as advertised on their website). My friend Conch had her Wedding Photography done at the Zoo and the photos are spectacular.

Getting there by Bus
Routes 30 & 31 run between Perth Busport (on Wellington St), Elizabeth Quay Bus Station and Perth Zoo's entrance [stop #11847]. Buses on these routes are low-floor/accessible. We recommend boarding at Elizabeth Quay Bus Station for the fastest journey between the Perth CBD and the Zoo (6 mins).

Perth Zoo opened its gates on 17 October 1898, welcoming 53,000 visitors in its first nine months of operation. Admission fees remained unchanged until 1951—a modest six pence for adults and three pence for children! When the 41-acre South Perth site was chosen in 1897, meticulous planning of the gardens became a priority. Head gardener Henry Steedman, together with Zoo founder Ernest Le Souef, dedicated countless hours to create a botanical haven. Cartloads of manure were brought in daily for two years to enrich the sandy, nutrient-poor soil. An artesian bore was sunk to irrigate the plants and trees sourced from all corners of the British empire.

A visit to Perth Zoo *today* presents a stark contrast to previous eras, even just a few decades ago. Perth's modern zoo boasts a dedicated team of 200 staff members committed to delivering exceptional experiences. Animals now thrive in appropriate social groups within naturalistic settings, with their welfare as the utmost priority. By exposing visitors to the wonders of the natural world, we aim to foster positive attitudes toward wildlife that benefit both society and the environment.

To realise our modern vision, significant changes were necessary. Outdated cement cages, bars, and mesh barriers that failed to meet contemporary animal welfare standards became a thing of the past. We replaced the elephants' concrete jungle with an environment reminiscent of their natural habitat. Where a picnic oval once stood, a sprawling and captivating African habitat emerged. We first moved the orangutans from confining cages, allowing them to explore open exhibits. Later, we constructed towering tree-like structures to provide them with elevated living spaces, aligning with their natural instincts.

The days of bars separating visitors from animals are gone. Instead, we employ subtler safety barriers such as moats, water bodies, and glass enclosures. Across the entire Zoo, industrial enclosures have given way to meticulously designed, naturalistic habitats tailored to meet the specific physical, psychological and social needs of our animal residents. As you immerse yourself in Perth Zoo's heritage and marvel at its transformation, remember that our journey continues. The future holds new exhibits, expansion projects and initiatives aimed at furthering our conservation and education efforts.

The role and purpose of zoos have changed enormously in recent decades. Perth Zoo – in collaboration with scientific agencies, governments and other conservation partners – plays a part in the much bigger picture of the conservation of our natural world. We contribute directly to the preservation of species and habitat diversity while also providing visitors with the opportunity to encounter the natural world and become involved in conservation.

30. CITY OF PERTH'S MUSEUM

The Western Australian Museum's long and fascinating history reflects and documents the State's rich and diverse natural and cultural heritage. The Western Australian Museum is the State's premier cultural organisation, housing WA's scientific and cultural collection.

For over 120 years the Museum has been making the State's natural and social heritage accessible and engaging through research, exhibitions and public programs.

Today, the Museum has seven public locations across our State – and a Collections and Research Centre that houses more than eight million objects.

The WA Museum Boola Bardip opened in the Perth Cultural Centre on Saturday 21 November 2020 with nine days of celebration.

Established in 1891 in the old Perth gaol, it was known as the Geological Museum and its collections were geological, ethnological and biological. In 1897 it officially became the Western Australian Museum and Art Gallery.

Travel Like a Local

During 1959 the botanical collection was transferred to the new Herbarium and the Museum and the Art Gallery became separate institutions. The Museum focused its collecting and research interests in the areas of natural sciences, anthropology, archaeology and the State's history. Over the 1960s and 1970s it also began to work in the emerging areas of historic shipwrecks and Aboriginal site management.

Today the Western Australian Museum comprises six public sites and a collection and research centre and houses more than 8 million objects from rare fossils to the iconic racing yacht *Australia II*.

The Museum also manages 200 shipwreck sites of the 1500 known to be located off the WA coast and manages eight Aboriginal land reserves. We recommend pre-purchasing tickets online for traveling exhibitions and during school holidays to avoid delays.

What's showing at the moment:

Meeyakba Shane Pickett: Six Seasons features a series of acclaimed works interpreting the Nyoongar six seasons and the landscape of the south-west of Western Australia. Born in Quairading, Ballardong Country, "Meeyakba" (Shane's Nyoongar name which translates to something like "light of the moon") Shane Pickett (1957 – 2010) is remembered as one of Western Australia's preeminent landscapes artists and one of the foremost Nyoongar artists of his generation. The seasons contain the signs that guide movement within country, indicate when resources are available and mark the rhythms of cultural and ceremonial life. Shane's work has been exhibited in every state and territory in Australia, as well as internationally, and been recognised in numerous major art awards.

Audio-visual works also present further insights into Shane's life and career and a contemporary interpretation of the six seasons by digital artist Sohan Ariel Hayes. The exhibition is a collaboration with the Mossenson Art Foundation, where Shane worked as an artist for the last decade of his career.

Check out our exhibition talk with Dr. Henry Skerritt: The art of Meeyakba Shane Pickett

Museum Bookings:
Book a ticket online or by calling 1300 134 081. This is recommended if you wish to visit on a particular day. Walk-up entry is available each day — no booking required! However, you may experience a wait time during busy periods such as weekends.

If you register for a tour or an event, admission is included in your booking.

31. CITY OF PERTH'S ART GALLERY

WA's Art Gallery is an *amazing* place to check out. You can either visit for a *gold coin donation* (you can literally just give a dollar if you're running low on cash) or you can pay more to attend more specialised shows.

The Western Australia Art Collection is housed in the museum which is located at the Perth Cultural Centre. The main gallery building was built in 1977 and features elements of Bauhaus architecture with a Brutalist exterior. At the time of construction the architectural design was considered innovative, but even now there's something modern and cool about the building itself.

The Western Australian collection has been accumulating since 1895 and the collection has evolved into an invaluable record of Western Australian history in a huge variety of drawings, paintings and prints. If you have the time, money and inclination; I recommend taking the "Western Australia's Paradise: A Private Day Tour From Perth". It's a great way to explore the gallery and learn about the artists.

32. DAY TRIPPIN' – ROCKINGHAM

After humble beginnings as a timber port in the 1870s, Rockingham has grown to become a fabulous day trip destination for families, nature lovers, and adventure junkies alike. Its location, less than 50 kilometres south of the Perth CBD — exactly 48 minutes by car — means it's convenient enough to go for a day trip, and so much on offer, that you'll want to stay for longer. Rockingham is a beautiful coastal city with access to Perth's beloved "Penguin Island" that hosts and cares for the cutest little fairy penguins in the world.

Situated less than 50 kilometres south of the Perth CBD, or 48 minutes by car to be exact, Rockingham — or *the Swinging Pig*, as it's affectionately termed — is known for its relaxed coastal vibe, pristine beaches, and flourishing wildlife. The name of the seaside town came from the sailing ship, Rockingham, one of the three vessels Thomas Peel chartered to carry settlers to Western Australia. In 1830, the ship was beached due to heavy weather and later abandoned after failed attempts to re-float her. So, whether you're keen to spend the day exploring one of the many offshore islands, try your hand at adrenalin-pumping adventure, or for a little R&R,

there's a bounty of ways to while away the hours in this charming coastal town.

Whether it's the glittering turquoise water, technicolour reefs, or ship-wrecked dotted coastline, when it comes to Rockingham, a day trip to Shoalwater Islands Marine Park is a must. And there's no better way to explore the enchanting island paradise than a wildlife snorkel tour.

Book in for a [Snorkel with Wild Sea Lions & Wildlife Adventure tour](#) with Perth Wildlife Encounters for a five-hour journey to the island's top snorkel spots where you'll experience the best of the local marine life, both above and below the water. You'll meet local bird life, swim alongside wild Bottlenose dolphins, and frolic with the world's rarest species of Sea Lion while exploring limestone reefs and rocky outcrops. You'll also get to nibble on a gourmet grazing platter, adorned with a delectable assortment of seafood to keep those hunger pangs at bay. The boat is fitted with wetsuits, floatation devices, and plenty of snorkel equipment to ensure loads of fun is had both on and under the water. Plus, the experienced crew will also introduce you to snorkelling with an emphasis on safety and environmental awareness, so you can get the most out of your encounter.

33. DAY TRIPPIN' – SWAN VALLEY: WHITEMAN PARK, WINE & BEER TOURS

You can either tour amazing Whiteman Park with the family and check out the various day shows where you can meet wombats, swing buckets of milk for baby cattle or give cracking a whip a go.

If wine and craft beers are more your thing, Swan Valley has some great tours where you can sample different wines and craft beers along with native Australian foods while getting some amazing experiences in Swan Valley's gorgeous vineyards.

The entire Swan Valley is made up of world-class wineries, breweries, distilleries, countless gourmet artisan goods, handcrafted wares, bustling markets, vibrant studios, top-notch eateries and endless experiences, just 25 minutes from Perth's city centre.

The Swan Valley is bathed in stunning sunshine for most of the year, making it the ideal region to visit during every season. Grape pickers and winemakers are at their busiest in the summer, where ripe, sun-drenched fruit gets picked and the winemaking process begins. In autumn, the mornings are crisp, the days are mild, and the grass starts to green. Expect slightly colder and rainier days in winter, but don't let it stop you from coming out and enjoying some decadent food or a warming glass of wine from one of the Valley's best restaurants, wineries or breweries. In spring, see the stunning Swan Valley at its best, where the sky stretches in a sea of endless blue and the grapevines are green and lush.

There's a reason why the finest artisans in the land call the Swan Valley home. Why world-class chefs travel thousands of miles across the globe to lay their roots here. Why brewers, chocolatiers, honey producers and ice-cream and nougat makers have set up shop here. Why leading vintners choose to plant their vines here. After all, this is a place where the earth is rich and fruit and vegetables ripen to perfection under a warm sun. Where grape varietals flourish. Where cows and poultry are raised with open space and kindness, creating succulent local meats.

Swan Valley is a place that takes its fresh produce seriously. It's steeped in First Nations and Mediterranean migration history, laden with the oldest vines in WA, with time-honoured recipes and generations of tradition and passion sown into the land. It's an artist's mecca too, with leading sculptors and fine artists setting up impressive studios and galleries here.

Ready to explore? It's time to hit over 150 attractions in the region, all accessible over a 32km loop. How slow you go, and whether you go by tour or car is completely up to you.

34. DAY TRIPPIN' – MANDURAH: THE MANDURAH GIANTS.

Mandurah is Perth's version of Venice. With a range of stunning watery canals, gorgeous shore-side cafes, pubs and restaurants, you'll want to dedicate some time to take in all of Mandurah's amazing sights and sounds. Originally known as *Mandjoogoordap*, Mandurah means *'meeting place of the heart'*. And once you arrive in Mandurah, it's easy to see why it was crowned Australia's Top Tourism Town in 2023. Take your time to leisurely enjoy Mandurah's stunning *waterways for days,* beautiful sea-side pubs, amazing marina-inspired stores and so much more.

As Western Australia's largest regional city, Mandurah is known for its beautiful waterways and relaxed holiday atmosphere. There is plenty of accommodation options to choose from and an excellent range of restaurants located along the estuary foreshore and the Mandurah Boardwalk.

Travel Like a Local

Covering an area twice the size of Sydney Harbour and regarded as one of Australia's most spectacular playgrounds for boating, fishing and wildlife watching, the Mandurah Estuary and Peel Inlet provide endless water-based activities.

For those who enjoy being on the water, no trip to Mandurah would be complete without a boat cruise through the canals - be sure to keep an eye out for the wild bottle-nosed dolphins who are regular visitors to the area. Graced with endless stretches of pristine coastline, tree lined walkways, grassed picnic areas, plenty of attractions and safe swimming beaches; Mandurah is a perfect holiday destination for the whole family.

What's even more awesome about Mandurah is that it's home to the ***Giants of Mandurah***. Created by the famous Danish recycling artist, Thomas Dambo, these huge, beautifully built wooden sculptures show off the artist's love for eco-friendliness and creativity.

They're like the eco-friendly guardians of Mandurah, protecting the city's awesome treasures, especially those internationally famous wetlands. Thanks to the incredible success of the Giants of Mandurah (we Perthies absolutely love finding and visiting the giants and feel especially proud when we find the 'secret giant' at the very end of the hunt), the exhibition has been extended beyond November 2023 and is expected to remain for another 3 years. To see the "*Mandurah Giants*" art pieces, you're gonna need a map, a clues booklet (from the Mandurah visitors centre) and a full tank of petrol. You can try to see them on your own (it will take a full day so have at least 8 hours set aside to give you time to find all the giants) or there are tours based on finding the Giants, so you can join in with a fun crew or you can take the booklet and find them in your time. (Images sourced from: https://visitmandurah.com/giants-of-mandurah-tours/).

35. DAY TRIPPIN' – FREMANTLE: FREO MARKETS & ISLAND HOPPING

Fremantle, fondly referred to by us locals as "Freo" is a dynamic, "hippie-style" (okay that's what we Northerners think) Port City. Freo gets regarded as Western Australia's "cultural epicentre" and is just 23 kilometres southwest of Perth's CBD. Freo city is built from historical architecture and promotes creativity and individuality; making it the home of many artisans, writers, musicians, and artists. Set on the idyllic Perth coastline, this seaside location is the place where the sea meets the city, fish and chips meet fine dining, maritime museums meet prestigious artworks, and where the best of beach life dances with the best of city life.

A sunny afternoon in Perth calls for a wander through the iconic **Fremantle markets**. Established in 1897, the markets are an ideal way to immerse yourself in the vibrant culture and heritage of the area and set out on a sensory journey. Stroll through the stalls brimming with fresh local produce, handcrafted goods, vintage finds, homewares, street food vendors, and so much more. Allow the scents of international flavours to fill the air around you as the gentle strums of a nearby busker's guitar add a melodic backdrop.

Every weekend, treat yourself to a feast of colour, flavours and sounds at the well-known Freo Markets. Just in 'test tastes' alone, you'll be full enough not to need to buy lunch. I love honeycake from the honey stand, bite-sized proffiterjes from the pancake stall and a really great Asian-fusion meal from the team at "Bali in Perth" in the food traders section of the markets. Nothing beats some satay and rice, am I right?

For an awesome way to spend half a day in Freo, I highly recommend securing a spot on a **Sailing Catamaran** (it's bright yellow and really beautiful) to **Carnac Island Tour** and begin your voyage to one of Fremantle's hidden treasures. The tour aboard the luxury catamaran lasts about four hours, giving you loads of time to curate your own experience with as much relaxation or adventure as you choose. As you sail along, feel the fresh, salty breeze in your hair as you depart the harbour and glide across the tranquil morning ocean. As you approach the secluded island, watch as the sea's gradient of colours transitions before you, from shades of deep midnight blue to glimmering aquamarine, before becoming crystal clear at the shoreline.

Travel Like a Local

Once you arrive at Carnac Island, the choice of how you spend your time is completely yours. Grab a kayak or stand-up paddleboard and explore life above the water, or put on a snorkel, dive below, and take in all the sights and feelings the underwater world has to offer. If keeping it more lowkey is your style, then you'll want to bask in the Catamaran's cargo net where you'll be able to absorb all the views. One sight you won't want to miss is the rarest sea lion in the world, the Australian sea lion. A colony of these adorable creatures use the island as a place of refuge between feeding. If they're not gliding past the Catamaran through the depths of the ocean, they'll no doubt be observing you from the sun-drenched sands of the island.

36. DAY TRIPPIN ROCKINGHAM PENGUIN ISLAND

Rockingham is about an hour's drive from Perth's city centre or over an hour's train ride from Perth's main Train station. Rockingham is a beautiful, peaceful seaside village and home to one of Perth's most amazing tourist spots; Penguin Island.

Blessed with white sandy beaches and surrounded by crystal clear waters, Penguin Island is just 40 minutes south of Perth and lies a five minute ferry ride away in the heart of the ruggedly spectacular Shoalwater Islands

Marine Park. The wildlife is the star attraction. Join us for a cruise to see wild dolphins and rare Australian sea lions before visiting beautiful Penguin island. Getting here is easy with ferries departing hourly from 9am to 3pm. Spend as long, or as little as you like to swim, snorkel, picnic and explore the nature trails and beaches before catching a return ferry at your leisure.

When you hop across on the ferry to Penguin Island, you'll be able to spend the day:

Swimming and snorkelling the crystal clear waters of Shoalwater Bay

Exploring the nature trails & boardwalks taking in spectacular views of the Marine Park

Having a picnic under the trees overlooking a safe swimming beach ideal for young children

Seeing nesting pelicans & other sea birds up close especially in September & October when the chicks are hatching.

Using the binoculars at the lookouts to spot dolphins & whales (September to December)

Penguin Island offers a wide range of tour options (swim with dolphins or snorkel with seals, stay overnight for their longest tour, have an amazing 'sunset tour' with a glass of bubbly champagne or set out on a kayak tour of the island) and each includes different highlights. The most popular option is the "Dolphins, Penguin Island and Sealions Cruise" which can be booked online through the Perth Wildlife Encounters website on this link: https://www.penguinisland.com.au/

On the Dolphins, Penguin Island and Sealions Cruise Tour, travellers can enjoy the scenic highlights of the Shoalwater Islands Marine Park and keep a look out for the wildlife! The tour's 1-hour glass bottom boat cruise takes place in the ruggedly spectacular coastlines of Penguin, Seal & Bird Islands and takes advantage of the best wildlife spotting opportunities of the day. Wild dolphins, rare Australian sea lions, pelican rookeries, and birds of prey are regularly sighted and our friendly crew will get you right amongst the action!

The cruise concludes on Penguin Island allowing for a 30-minute guided wildlife walk of Penguin Island, providing exclusive insight into the local penguins, the spectacular landscapes and the natural history of the island and if you have more time then you can enjoy swimming, snorkelling, exploring the nature trails or just relax and enjoy the beautiful nature reserve. Before returning on the ferry at your own leisure.

Perth Wildlife tours can also organise specialised group tours to Penguin Island or even help you plan an incredible Wedding there if you want to. The choices are endless, and it all looks like an amazing way to spend the day.

37. WEEKEND ROADTRIP – CALL SHOTGUN ON THE WAY TO BUSSLETON

OK, Perth locals call it "*Busso*". Bussleton is a beautiful sea-side village about 2 hour's drive south of Perth.

The Western Australia "*Walking on a Dream*" site (2023) explains how: "Busselton sits at the top end of the famous wine region of Margaret River – it's only 23 minutes' drive to Dunsborough, or 42 minutes' drive to Margaret River township, with cellar doors, restaurants and vineyards dotted along the way. The drive to Busselton from Perth takes roughly 2.5 hours. Or, you could fly, with the Busselton Margaret River Airport sitting 6.5 kilometres from the town centre, equipped for everything from A330s to private aircraft"

When you arrive at Busso, you'll want to take a quick dip in *Geographe Bay*, a calm cove that has usually still and shallow waters; just right for taking little ones or for dipping your legs in without having to commit to full submersion. For an ice-cold pint, Busso is also home to Shelter Brewing Co., a new addition to a growing number of local beer brewers. Sip a local pale ale within sight of the little ones and watch for whales blowing and breaching

Travel Like a Local

on the horizon.

Busselton is a place that's on the move with artisanal food, produce and craft destination.

The Bussleton Jetty was built in 1865 and is the Southern Hemisphere's *longest timber jetty* (at almost 2kms) and probably WA's prettiest, too. It's a long walk and an incredible experience to be on the decked area but also in the middle of the sea.

For little ones or the elderly or impaired, a cute little train goes up and down the jetty throughout the day. The depths of the Indian Ocean are so far out that the Busselton Jetty was repeatedly extended, that's why it's so long. At its end, find an underwater observatory with enormous windows placing you alongside colourful coral, patterned fish and the occasional turtle. For a fairly reasonable fee, visitors get to descend several floors below the waterline while staying perfectly dry. The view of all the coloured fish and pretty coral is worth taking a peek. Busso has a lively 'beachy' town centre with loads of quaint stores, cafes and places to play. The more than 150-year-old jetty faces a grassy, playground-filled foreshore, where kids can get sprinkled with water falling from a whale's tail, scale ropes up a life-sized shipwreck and clamber over a giant octopus; making Bussleton a perfect place for a weekend family getaway.

38. WEEKEND ROADTRIP – CALL SHOTGUN ON THE WAY TO MARGARET RIVER

Margs. *Happy sigh*. That's what we locals call our beloved "Margaret River" wine region. Going to Margs with my husband is one of my *favourite* things to do throughout the year. We'll hustle hard at work, then book time off over a long weekend to rest, recharge and reconnect with each other in Margs. Margaret River is the home of the most beautiful vineyards, wineries and breweries in the whole of Western Australia. It's wonderful to escape Perth's heat in the summer and go on a road trip "down south" to Margs where cooler weather, lush, evergreen forests and beautiful thornless, fragrant roses in all colours and sizes await.

The Margaret River Region is an area of magnificent beauty on the Southwest Coast of the beautiful state of Western Australia. Stretching from Busselton along the shores of Geographe Bay down to Augusta the most south-westerly point of Australia. The area abounds with spectacular beaches, exquisite caves, adventurous walks and trails, world class surfing spots, welcoming locals, divine cuisine and award winning wine in nearly every direction!

Travel Like a Local

Margs' stunning coastline spans an area of over 100kms, overlooking the magnificent Indian Ocean, making it a perfect holiday destination as you tour and explore.

Visitors from around the planet have been charmed by their visit to the Margaret River Region, the ancient land of the Noongar people for over 40,000 years. It is steeped in history with impressive ancient landforms, cliffs, beaches, forests, headlands, rocks and sunsets that will last forever in your mind.

The towns of the region each provide their own enticing reasons to visit. The locals really enjoy living in this wonderful part of the planet, living a relaxing and peaceful life surrounding with natural beauty and wonderful weather most of the year round!

So many marvellous views to enrich your experience of being alive and all within such a compact geographical area makes the Margaret River region a 'Jewel in the Crown', attracting millions of visitors every year from all around the world.

Discovering the Margaret River Region by car, camper, bike or foot is easy and relaxed. Choose to vary your surroundings by staying a few nights in one place and moving to another, roaming around to maximise your holiday experience. Or find the location you resonate with the most and relax there for a while, both ways will add up to a perfect holiday for people of all ages.

In the Margaret River region, life is celebrated and enjoyed. Whether you're in Busselton, Dunsborough, Yallingup, Margaret River or Augusta, the south west lifestyle is marvellous.

It's relaxing to spend time in an area of spectacular natural beauty alongside the peaceful locals, rejuvenating your mind, body and spirit!

Outstanding areas of natural beauty abound. Margs is a place of ancient forests, inviting clear blue ocean with white sandy shores, caves of wonder, formidable rock formations, walking, biking and 4WD trails, wildlife and wildflowers. Blessed with a temperate climate all year round and heat in the summer and surrounding months it makes this a very popular tourist destination.

With an eclectic mix of small and large towns, each offering their own flavour, together they have created a region that is overflowing with possibility for visitors. Many people say it is some of the nicest weather on the coast; it's definitely a nice break from the searing heat of Perth's city and suburbs in summer.

Travel Like a Local

Margaret River started out famous for surfing, but has now added world class wine, gourmet cuisine, artisan wares and unique attractions to the list of reasons to visit. Marg's WA region is beautiful from top to bottom, waves to caves, from Cape Naturaliste to Cape Leeuwin - the northern cape where the southern ocean meets Geographe Bay along the northern coast of the Margaret River region is an amazing sight, and the rocks and waves of the Naturaliste peninsula must be seen to be believed.

The coast south from Yallingup to Prevelley is spectacular, and so is the surfing! Dozens of divine beaches offer fishing, swimming, boating, paddling, snorkelling, diving, kiting and relaxing opportunities. Spot whales in season or swim with the dolphins. Choose rock climbing, abseiling, horse riding, cycling, kayaking, bush walking, spelunking and skydiving, it's all available in the Margaret River Region and what's more - a *stunning* Insta-worthy backdrop comes as standard feature of beautiful Margs.

The southern tip at Cape Leeuwin is steeped in the history of the Western Australian seafaring past.
Caves offer a glimpse into ancient depths and show the growth of rocks over thousands of years. Wonderous sights; Margs really has it all.

Catering for tourists for many years the people in the region are adept at making you feel welcome whether you are a business or leisure traveller, and people return again and again to experience the infamous Margaret River Region hospitality. The foreshores of all the towns along the coast in Margs are well designed and offer leisure and recreational facilities of the highest quality. Ample parking and regular play parks throughout the towns are all reasons the region is a good place to visit.

As for families visiting Margs, kids of all ages love an adventure amongst the rocks, sand and sea, and the inspiring sights are great for all ages. A great selection of man-made attractions can educate and entertain young ones while being part of an activity that is interesting and inspiring including lighthouses, the underwater observatory, mazes, fun parks, caves and forest walks.

Foodies and wine lovers are able to indulge their senses with gourmet local produce.

Wine, beer and ciders of distinction; sweet treats of chocolate, fudge, nougat, ice cream; cheese, nuts, yoghurts and oils and freshly grown Farmers Market produce plus numerous other culinary delights await your arrival. Cafés, bistros, restaurants, beach bars, good old fashioned fish & chips, raw, gluten free and vegetarian choices, tea shops, sushi bars, delicatessens, mobile coffee bars, bakeries and

Travel Like a Local

more offer a range of high quality food and drink to be enjoyed throughout the day and night.

Nature lovers resonate with this piece of Earth's paradise. The abundance of trails, including the region's Cape to Cape trail along the coastline, provide exhilarating outdoor walking experiences many with mesmerising coastal and inlet views. Explore the world's last remaining Tuart Forest or meander in the solitude of the towering Boranup Karri forest trees for absolute peace and tranquility.

39. WEEKEND ROADTRIP – CALL SHOTGUN ON THE LONG DRIVE DOWN TO ALBANY – VIA PEMBERTON

This is probably one of the longest drives and I recommend putting aside a week for this trip so you can enjoy at your leisure and not be stressed about driving 5 hours down South and making it back in time for work on Monday or Tuesday morning.

The beautiful Princess Royal Harbour and King George Sound surround the City of Albany in the Great Southern, a historically significant region of Western Australia. The King George Sound was the site of Western Australia's first European settlement, settled several years before the Swan River Colony in Perth. Albany's safe anchorages attracted many sailing ships in the early years of exploration of the Australian coastline. European settlement began in 1826 and Albany grew into a thriving port during the 19th and 20th centuries. It served as a gateway to the Eastern Goldfields and, for many years, it was the colony's only deep-water port and a place of importance for shipping services between Britain and its Australian colonies.

The waterways around Albany have continued to be significant to the town's trade, with whaling being an important industry in the early 20th century, and Albany now being a prominent spot to watch migrating humpback and southern right whales along the dramatic coastline. Tours depart from the harbour between June and August.

When Alun and I spent a week in Albany last Autumn, we were blown away by how gorgeous and friendly the seaside city centre is. I felt right at home in the quaint bookstores and cafes while Alun enjoyed making a few new mates over a beer at one of Albany's 4 pubs in the town centre. It's great to be able to walk around shops, cafes and pubs and be able to see the sea from every window. Albany's town centre has a wonderful community feel and it's nice being out and about and

Travel Like a Local

seeing friends wave to each other and store owners greeting locals by name.

Albany is the best place for seeing WA's amazing natural attractions, too. Alun and I travelled out to see the "Gap and natural wonders" which were amazing to see. The surging power of the Southern Ocean is evident at The Gap, a spectacular channel in the 40-metre high coastal granites of Torndirrup National Park. Lookouts at both the Gap and natural Bridge provide outstanding views of the Southern Ocean and the coast from Bald Head to West Cape Howe. Visitors to the Gap can venture onto a universally accessible new viewing platform directly above the surging seas in all but the worst weather conditions. From the gentle and mesmerising heaving of calm seas to the buffeting rush of wind and spray of winter storms, the experience changes from day to day. A raised pathway leads from the car-park and picnic area across the top of the exposed granite ramparts to reach the viewing platform at the Gap. The pathway gives safe access to the best views while protecting vulnerable plants and lichens on the rock surface from trampling.

Personally, as someone who suffers with mental illness, it was touching to see that along the drive from Albany Town Centre to the Gap, there were loads of signs encouraging people to reach out if they needed help and posters of critical life-saving organisations.

40. ADVENTURES YOU NEED A WEEK TO SEE. MAYBE A PLANE, TOO

Heading over to Karijini is probably one of the longest drives you'll take, so I recommend putting aside a week for this trip so you can enjoy at your leisure and not be stressed about driving 7 hours "down South" and making it back in time for work on Monday or Tuesday morning. Albany is an absolutely gorgeous sea-side city and worth going to see but it's about a 5-6 hour drive down south so I also recommend getting an hour's flight instead so you can let loose and enjoy Albany's beautiful sites and places to grab a meal or a cold beer without having to drive all those hours back to Perth's city centre.

Or you can book flights and head "up North" to Broome for a long weekend and enjoy everything that beautiful Broome has to offer. Even though Broome is in the same state as Perth; it's like another country when you arrive. It feels like 'real Australia' when you're surrounded in burnt-red lands with turquoise seas. It's next level and has an amazing, chilled atmosphere. When my husband and I headed out to Broome for a week's holiday, we were amazed by the stunning landscapes it offered **and were equally surprised at how hard taxis are to catch**. They're not really known for reliable taxis there so talk to some of the locals or ask some Perth peeps before heading out to Broome – people can put you in touch with 'drivers' they've used in the past and these will come in handy if you go out for the night and need to get back to your hotel safely.

41. PERTH'S NIGHT FEVER NIGHTLIFE

This part of the travel guide I had to research because I'm part of the Perth population that is home and in bed – asleep – by 9:30pm every evening. I'm not sure what goes on at night because I'm in my 40's and want to be in my pjs at home rather than tearing it up in Nightclubs or Bars. I'm old. I like my sleep.

If you *do* want to go out late at night, though – here are some cool places to check out.

Somewhere in Northbridge's China Town lies **"Sneaky Tony's"** prohibition rum bar. You'll need a password to be let into this funky, hidden away (literally) pub, but if you sign up to join "Sneaky Tony's Facebook" page on this link: (https://www.facebook.com/sneakytonys/), they'll let you know what the password for that night is and you'll be in amongst all the cool cats. With over 300 different bottles of rum gathered from the four corners of the world, you'll find something just right for your tastes at Sneaky Tony's.

If having fun after sundown makes you happy, then read on. From vibrant nightclubs to elegant wine bars and jazz clubs; chatter-filled pubs to magnificent concert halls and stately theatres, you'll be spoilt for choice in Perth.

The "*MyGuide Perth*" (2023) website recommends heading out for an evening in Northbridge "*with its wide selection of cafes, restaurants, nightclubs and bars. Good entertainment also can be found in Mount Lawley, Subiaco and Leederville. Further afield is Fremantle, home to many talented artists and musicians, some of whom are now international stars; excellent live music is aplenty here!*" They do warn that "Nightspots in Northbridge can get pretty busy and rowdy during the weekend and on the eve of public holidays, so remember not to drink and drive and definitely keep your wits about you as the night gets later.

Perth's nightlife is generally relaxed and centred on pubs and small bars. Whether you're after wine, gin, rum, whiskey, or craft beer, Perth has got you covered. For bar-hopping, head to Northbridge and explore the neighbourhoods' hidden speakeasies. Be warned: a cocktail at one of these trendy establishments doesn't come cheap – bring your wallet and be prepared for some high-priced cocktails. Pubs, also called hotels, can be found in every neighbourhood, often staying open from midday to midnight and acting as a meeting place for the local community. We *sandgropers* love our home-grown bands which can be discovered at some of Perth's trendiest bars in Leederville, Subiaco or even along the Vic Park café strip. You could also catch the train down to Freo of an evening and popping into one of their bars for some live bands and reminders of great rock songs. As a Northerner though – I tend to lean more towards musicians North of the river, just saying. On Thursday, Friday, and Saturday nights, visitors to Perth can discover a thriving after-dark scene in the neighbourhoods of Northbridge, Leederville, and Mount Lawley. Most pubs and bars are open until midnight, while the larger clubs are busiest between 10:00 pm and 2:00 am

42. "SWEET, BRO" PERTH'S TASTIEST DESSERTS

I don't know about you, but there's a special place in *my* stomach reserved for dessert. Dessert is soul food. It's comforting and there's something really special about finding a sweet treat that really hits the spot. For desserts in Perth, the best place to access a load of different options is Northbridge. Walking to Northbridge is easy from either the main Perth Train Station or down the big steps from the Perth Cultural Centre – where the Library, Art Gallery and Museum are.

A quick stroll to Northbridge gives you access to these amazing dessert places:

Grab an amazing dessert at Whisk Creamery – Is located at 246 William Street, Northbridge. The team at Whisk Creamery take dessert to the next level with their dessert-only menu. You can try some really cool new flavours; including their Easter-Themed "Hot cross bun Gelato" (I'm writing this guide during Easter so that's the special this month), their house made mango and passionfruit sorbet or my favourite – their "Unicorn" ice-cream dessert made from their creamy vanilla gelato, an edible unicorn horn, colourful sprinkles and flamed marshmallow. It not only looks like every little girl's dream – it tastes amazing. Whisk offers 12 'in house special' ice-creams and rotates/creates a new special every month – you'll have to check them out to find out what's new on your visit. Whisk also does the yummiest "Cronut" (half croissant, half donut) sandwiches with loads of their specialty flavoured ice-cream.

Comfort yourself after a long day with a thick, incredible Spanish hot chocolate and light, fluffy Spanish churros from **San Churros on James Street**, Northbridge. When you can put your teaspoon into your hot chocolate and it stays upright for a good few seconds, you know you're onto something special. Something delicious. I used to work in Northbridge and after a really tough day, I'd pop into San Churro and order their Spanish hot chocolate (it's out of this world good) and their classic "Churros for one". It cheered me up every time. San Churros is a perfect place to go for some classic Spanish desserts; with churros, cakes, ice cream and a wide selection of gourmet chocolates on offer. If you lean more towards the savoury, San Churros has expanded its menu to include a few Spanish tapas options, too. I think a combination of something sweet (Spanish hot chocolate) with something warm and savoury (their melted cheese toastie is pretty good) is a great way to brighten the evening.

Stop and get a huge, delicious pretzel from the cute little **"Pretzels"** caravan in the centre of Perth's art district. The girls running the pastel-pink Pretzels van (it's so cute!) are the owners, so they put their heart and soul into creating and providing Perth's best pretzels. When you buy from these girls, you're supporting local business and feeding the dreams of young hard-working entrepreneurs.

For more dessert options, the "Visit Perth" (2023) website recommends 5 fairly new and pretty amazing places to stop by for incredible desserts in Northbrige: "Cult favourite *"Kuld Creamery"* has added to the abundance of ice cream options in the city with their new store on Roe Street. These guys believe 'less is more' and release just a handful of flavour options at a time, so you'll find something different there each month (including vegan options made with cashew cream and organic coconut milk). No matter when you visit, you can expect some seriously good flavour combos studded with sweet extras and swirled with sauces. Try a scoop in a cookie sandwich for a real treat. At **"Cuccini Gelato"** on William Street in Northbridge, the team are busy churning up sweet sensations in an authentic Italian gelato machine. There are classic flavours like milk chocolate gelato and lemon sorbet, of course, but if you're after something a bit different – keep an eye out for quirkier options like saffron; their crazy 'avo and lime' (It's a wild flavour to try, right?); or even their 'cucumber and mint' gelato! Everything is made from scratch and these guys at Cuccini are open from midday until late seven days a week. I'm a simple girl, so I don't tend to stray far from vanilla-bean gelato for dessert, but one of my best friends "G" prefers a more "grown-up" after-dinner indulgence, and loves ordering Cuccini's affogato with his choice of gelato (usually hazelnut).

Travel Like a Local

"**Muffle**" (a *muffle* is a chewy waffle wrapped into a cone shape) have also chosen William Street for their second shop. Their specialty is the 'muffle', a crispy, chewy waffle wrapped into a cone shape so you can carry it in one hand. These are filled with your choice of ice cream and toppings. From milo to matcha, there's an array of different flavoured fillings catering to every craving. The team at "Muffle" have also just recently introduced Kakigori; a Japanese shaved ice dessert which is a refreshing option for hotter days here in Perth; especially on a balmy summer's night.

"**Lucky Puffs**" has burst onto Perth's dessert scene; "levelling up" from a market food truck to an entire store on James Street. Their namesake puffs are fresh, fluffy pancake bites filled with custard, which you can enjoy laden with your favourite toppings (berries, nuts, sprinkles, sauces - you name it!). They also offer gluten-free and dairy-free 'likelets' (little pikelets) to cover a range of dietary requirements.

Last but not least - and not to be confused with Lucky Puffs - there's "**Lightning Puff**" - an artisan patisserie right off Aberdeen Street which offers exquisite éclair with different flavours each month. (*Can you even imagine? I bloody love a good éclair, me*). Their freshly-baked choux pastries are finished with creamy fillings and decadent toppings. The team at "Lightning Puff" offer different flavours each month, with the current offerings including a classic dark chocolate and a mojito-inspired apple, mint and lime creation... *mmm*. Lightning Puff is only open Wednesday to Saturday from 11am to 4pm or until sold out, so aim to arrive early for these yummy goodies.

43. PERTH'S PRETTIEST PUBS

I'm a non-drinker, so I'm usually the most sensible when it comes to nights out with my friends or with my husband and our mutual mates. Alcohol isn't that important to me (clearly), but a pretty drink with a great taste *and the location of the pub* is paramount. For me, being by water is the ultimate place to be when it comes to sharing tasty beverages with the people I love most.

Just some pro tips here – for some reason we call Pubs "hotels" here in Perth. You'll see a lot of things like "The Guildford Hotel" "The Bayswater Hotel" "The Civic Hotel" but they're probably not great places to stay. It's our 'code' for pub so don't let that throw you; and no, I don't recommend using one of these as accommodation on your trip to Perth.

Travel Like a Local

The Claisebrook Inlet in East Perth is home to the OG **"The Royal"** pub. (There's a new "The Royal" pub on William Street in the city but it doesn't come close to how pretty the original version is). On a summer's day, the inlet is like a mini-Venice and is the prime place to be with your mates. As you're sipping on ice-cold beers or pretty cocktails (ok "mocktails" for me), you can watch beautiful ships cruise in and out and if they're working on the days you're out, you can even see people catching gondolas up and down the river.

Here in Perth, we're all pretty spoilt for choice when it comes to bars along the coastline, but it's hard to go past the super pretty views at **Scarborough Beach Bar** (located at 1 Manning Street, Scarborough). Head straight upstairs to get a 'primo viewing' platform of surfers over the hill as you eat amazing 'coastal' inspired meals all set to chilled DJs, a very tempting cocktail selection and a wide range of beers on tap.

"Coast" Port Beach Bar in Fremantle is a gorgeous "totes casual" beach-side pub with *spectacular* ocean views from every table. The team at Coast boast as having "Perth's best fish and chips" so you might have to visit and test their amazing meal out. My husband has stopped here a few times for a cold beer on his marathon walks to Fremantle every January and his photos are stunning. The menu has all the local's fave meals, and the views are the best I've seen in Perth (okay, apart from the C Restaurant – but it's hard to beat a rotating restaurant). *Coast* is very proud of its *minimal environmental footprint* as being the only large event venue with *no single use plastic*. Coast's awesome focus on sustainability places them at the forefront of the environmental venues in Australia. The Coast team are big on recycling, are fully solar powered (come on now, this is awesome), and don't use straws, balloons, or any plastic items that might end up on the beautiful Port beach.

Since opening at the end of 2019, **The gorgeous "Beach House" pub** is just 100m from the beach in Jindalee and has fast become a real destination venue. The unmatched views are matched by the leafy, coastal interior decor, a cruisey coastal attitude and an awesome range of tap beers. Locals think it's definitely worth jumping in the car for a northern road trip to visit "*The Beach House*". *The Beach House* team boast: "Come for the breezy oceanfront location, stay for fridges packed with the craftiest choices and inventive takes on absolute staple dishes." *The Beach House* is a local spot – great for catching up with mates, diving into a long lunch or having dinner with the family. The Beach House menu is designed to be shared, but you can eat it any way you want to. Gluten free and vegan options are also available; they're an inclusive bunch at the Beach House. Their menu can be looked at online and is always changing. *The Beach House* menu also includes the exciting "*feed me*" option with a Chef-created menu for guests based on seasonal ingredients and what's the most amazing thing to eat at the time.

44. "BEACH ME OFF" – SCARBOROUGH BEACH

Or what we locals refer to as "Scabs". Good old Scabs is our *favourite* beach in Perth. When you get there, you'll see why. Scarborough has recently had a tonne of money poured into it and the results are WA's only incredible sparkly beach-side pool, the really cool new children's "Whale Bones" playground, the awesome new "Snake Pit" skate park and the beach's beautiful amphitheatre layout which is awesome for watching and supporting our "little nippers" on beach carnivals and sports days. The Amphitheatre is a great place for visitors to enjoy a picnic and watch the sunset. It is also the home of many events during the year, including the Thursday Night Markets during the summer.

Scarborough Beach has an active town centre with loads of places to eat and is lined with an array of sea-side pubs. It's loads of fun to go to and is always super busy during the summer months. Scarborough Beach is a vibrant stretch of coastline with bustling pedestrian promenades, a children's adventure playground, art projects, variety of skate bowls, climbing wall, half-court basketball, exercise equipment, amphitheatre and magnificent Sunset Hill. There are many cafés, bars, restaurants and shops and a large range of accommodation from backpacker hostels, affordable family apartments to luxury hotels with ocean views. Once you're done surfing, sunbathing and swimming spend a relaxing hour or two at one of the many cafés or bars overlooking the ocean. Or you can stay overnight, at one of the many accommodation options. During summer enjoy live entertainment at the only amphitheatre on the beach in WA.

45. "BEACH ME OFF" – COTTESLOE BEACH

Cottesloe Beach, or 'Cott/Cotts', as the locals call it, has long been one of Perth's prettiest beaches. It's pure white sand which stretches more than a kilometre along the coast meets impossibly blue water that's cherished for its swimming, surfing and snorkelling. Relax under the shady Norfolk Pines, snorkel amid a colourful reef, and dine overlooking the Indian Ocean in the iconic "Indiana Teahouse". My husband Alun is a *huge* Rugby fan, and he says that Cottesloe beach's Rugby pitch is one of the best

Travel Like a Local

he's ever seen – with a perfect view over our turquoise waves and sparkling white sand.

Cottesloe's crystal-clear ocean and colourful reefs invite ocean lovers all year round. When you get to Cottesloe, head to the protected waters at Peters Pool - North Cottesloe Beach with your snorkel or on a calm day, go looking for the endangered leafy sea dragon at South Cottesloe. If swimming is your thing, float in between the red and yellow beach flags and catch the waves all afternoon. Cottesloe is the birthplace of surfing and surf lifesaving in Western Australia, so it's no surprise that surfers flock to Cottesloe every day for a taste of its waves.

Before sunset, Perth locals gather together on picnic mats with friends and family to watch the stunning sunset over Cottesloe beach's pristine sand and waves. Instagram is alight with incredible photos of the sunset over Cottesloe and the best part is, every evening is different. No two sunsets are the same and locals gather regularly to eat fish and chips or sample some gorgeous ice-cream flavours from the bars, cafes and gelato stores just across the road from the beach's main entrance.

46. "BEACH ME OFF" – CITY & TRIGG BEACHES

City Beach used to be my husband's favourite beach for his "smoko" (Aussie for a "work lunch break") when he was an oven cleaner. It's easy to get to, really pretty and a lot quieter than Scarborough Beach. Even though City Beach is generally quieter than our other beaches, it offers all public amenities like toilets, showers, change rooms and has BBQ facilities situated on the grassed area directly above the beach. There's a huge playground for the kids, and in the summer months visitors can enjoy the free beach volleyball nets. Head past the northern groyne to the next bay to walk your beloved pets at the dog-friendly beach.

Sunset (and cocktail) lovers you can perch up at ultra-stylish Hamptons or Odyssea beach restaurants to enjoy quality food and beverage. For something a bit more family friendly 'Clancy's Fish Pub' offers a relaxed beachy atmosphere. City Beach Surf Life Saving Club patrol the beach in the summer months, with a surf lifesaving tower at the end of the southern groyne as an extra level of surveillance.

Trigg beach is the place to go for a quieter, calmer beach experience. Trigg beach also attracts more kite surfers than the other beaches with its perfect surfing conditions throughout most of the year.

Trigg is home to Perth's most consistent surf break, with local spots like Waterman's Bay, Mettams Pool (which is awesome for snorkelling) and Trigg Point also renowned for their surf. You can also play a round of golf at nearby, Joondalup Resort and explore many nature reserves and parks.

47. "BEACH ME OFF" – COOGEE BEACH

Where Scarborough is the popular extrovert at the party, Coogee is the quiet geek-but-sheek one towards the back, quietly surveying the party and taking it all in at a much slower pace. Coogee is a lesser-known beach, but an *amazing one* all the same. The wooden jetty is so much fun to jump off and the pretty inlet surrounded by rocks and coral protects it from big waves and makes it one of the more calm (waveless) beaches and perfect for paddleboarding or taking little ones to without fear they'll get knocked over by waves.

Although it's understated, Coogee Beach seems to attract the upper-end of Perth society so if you're going there, make sure you take your more fancy swimsuit and clad yourself in designer clothes and sunglasses.

48. STRIP IT DOWN – PERTH'S NUDIST BEACHES

Journalist Sean Goedecke from *Weekend Notes*'s website (2023) happily promotes being utterly at one with your unclothed body, stating: "*Nudism: we all practice it, some just wear clothes on top. Even in situations where clothes are unnecessarily restrictive or inconvenient – really hot days at the beach, lounging around at home, or long days at work – most of us bow to social pressure and button up our shirts. Here's a good general rule: make sure that you know a beach is empty (or that the people there are 'totes okay' with nudism) before you strip off.*"

Within sixty kilometres of Perth are two nude beaches, which you'll be welcome at so long as you follow nudist etiquette: don't litter, don't take unsolicited photographs or have sex, and if your bum's bare, throw a towel on the chair. Whether you're a first-time naturist or whether you're well acquainted with North Swanbourne Beach, the Western Australian Nudist Community has a lot to offer you – and nothing to hide.

North Swanbourne Beach is only a 30-minute drive from Perth's CBS and is one of the most popular nude beaches in WA, despite its technically-illegal status - apparently there are rules against being nude at the beach. LOL.

Travel Like a Local

North Swanbourne's 'nude bathing' area is about 300 metres north of the car park - which is *not* a nude zone, so if you're headed there for a visit, make sure you're past an official "clothing optional" sign before you strip off. The water is relatively waveless, so despite the lack of lifeguards, swimming should be safe for the whole family. The nude section of Warnbro Beach is almost a kilometre long, clearly marked, and shielded by a line of sand dunes.

49. TAKE A DRIVE ALONG PERTH'S AMAZING COASTLINE

If you've got time on a beautiful summer's eve – before the sun sets – I highly recommend hopping in the car and following the brown Tourist signs for the "Sunset Drive" along Perth's stunning coastline. On those lazy days, get out of the house in the comfort of your car to cruise through Perth's most mesmerising landscapes.

We have great weather almost year-round here in Perth, so roll your window down and fill your lungs with salty air as you drive the length of Perth's coastline. Start your journey in Cottesloe with an early morning dip and an Il Lido coffee to go before heading north along Marine Parade past early morning joggers and swimmers. Travel along West Coast Highway to City Beach. Stop at the lookout spot on **Reabold Hill** (the highest point along

Perth's coastline), where you will get sweeping views of Perth city and the surrounding areas from the highest natural point along the coast. Continue north past famous Scarborough Beach - a great place to stop for morning tea by the beach.

Just past Scarborough, make sure you turn off West Coast Highway on to **the West Coast Scenic Drive**. This will take you past the protected bays and beaches of the Sunset Coast to Hillarys Boat Harbour. Along the way you'll find some stunning photo opportunities, particularly at **Mettams Pool** and **Sorrento Beach**. Stop at Hillarys to visit AQWA to learn more about our underwater environment. Explore the network of boardwalks filled with shops and restaurants - this is a good spot to stop for lunch overlooking the harbour. In Summer, Hillarys Boat Harbour has safe swimming for families and the Great Escape offers fun activities for kids including waterslides, rides and mini golf.

Jump back in the car and keep heading north following the tourist drive signs Mullaloo Beach towards Mindarie, which is Australia's largest man-made marina and is a great place to end your journey. Stroll the Mediterranean-style boardwalks that lead you to cafés and restaurants where you can enjoy a local brew at the microbrewery. You can end your driving tour along the coastline with a picnic, or early dinner at the marina by the beach watching the sky transform with colour as the sun sinks slowly into the Indian Ocean.

50. "TIME TO GO" – IDEAS FOR GIFTS TO TAKE HOME WITH YOU THAT ARE UNIQUE TO PERTH

So, here it is. Your very last day in "The City of Lights".

If you fancy it, you can spend your last day exploring the attractions right in Perth's city centre, or you can have a more relaxing day at one of our beautiful beaches or parks. This is a great time to confirm your flights, make sure you have all your documents and passport ready and a great time to spend the day stretching your legs on a long walk or maybe cycling around the city and surrounds so you can work out before sitting for ages on your long plane trip home.

When thinking of gifts for those you love, Perth has some amazing unique-to-Perth souvenirs you can take home with you. A personalised coin from the Perth mint makes a wonderful gift, bottles of organic wine from the Wineries within the Swan Valley or dotted all over

Margaret river are also wonderful to gift with and for little ones, a soft toy version of our Perth Quokkas are a really cute idea. Market stalls and small shops around Perth and Freo offer Perth-based organic honey which can also make a thoughtful gift for the 'foodie' friend at home, or you can take back some original artworks or prints.

Wanting to help with this Travel Guide, my husband Alun wanted me to tell you that "the best gift you'll take away with you from Perth are the memories". Bless his heart. Hang onto those sun-dappled days of adventure during your trip to Perth and know that anytime you want to come back, we'll be happy to have you.

REFERENCES:

"*Alex Hotel*" review (2022) sourced (and re-written) from "*Luxury Hotel World*" in February 2024 from website: https://luxuryhotel.world/hotel/1418332

Beatty Lodge (2023) material sourced in March 2024 from website: https://beattylodge.com.au/

Best Nightlife in Perth (2023). Material sourced in March 2024 from: https://www.myguideperth.com/nightlife

Casey, Alexandra (2023). *Rockingham Day Trip: A Day of Adventure and Relaxation* on "So Perth" material sourced from: https://soperth.com.au/day-trip/rockingham-day-trip-a-day-of-adventure-and-relaxation

Choose your Pass, Choose your Adventure (2023) material sourced from Australia's Southwest: https://www.australiassouthwest.com/destinations/albany/

Ceccato, Monique (2023) *Perth's Sunset Tourist Drive* sourced online in March 2024 from: https://rac.com.au/travel-touring/info/scenic-drives-perth

"*Founding of Perth*" (May 2023) material sourced from *National Museum of Australia* accessed on 3rd Feb 2024 from website: https://www.nma.gov.au/defining-moments/resources/founding-of-perth#.

Genef, Kyla (2023). *Fremantle Day Trip: Exploring Perth's other Island hotspot.* Sourced from "So Perth" in March 2024 from: https://soperth.com.au/day-trip/fremantle-day-trip-exploring-perths-other-island-hotspot

Genef, Kyla. (2023) *Kings Park Day Trip: Discovering Perth's Urban Oasis* – So Perth Website sourced in March 2024 from: https://soperth.com.au/day-trip/kings-park-day-trip-discovering-perths-urban-oasis

Goedeck, Sean (2023)*The Best Nude Beaches in Perth* article sourced in March 2024 from website: https://www.weekendnotes.com/the-3-best-nude-beaches-near-perth/

Hayes, Chelsea *(2023). Five New Northbridge Spots for Sweet Treats.* Material sourced in March 2024 from "Visit Perth's" website: https://visitperth.com/en/blog/five-new-northbridge-spots-for-sweet-treats

McLaughlin, Molly (2023). *Nightlife in Perth: Best Bars, Clubs and More.* Featured on "Trip Savvy" and sourced in March 2024 from: https://www.tripsavvy.com/guide-to-nightlife-in-perth-4797410

Mandurah is the Perfect Base for Exploring the Mandurah and Peel Region. Sourced from 'Destination Perth' in March 2024 from: https://www.destinationperth.com.au/explore-perth/mandurah-and-peel/mandurah/

"*Snakes in Perth*" (2023) material sourced from *Snake Catcher, Perth* accessed on 3rd Feb 2024 from website: https://www.snakecatcherperth.com.au/snakes-perth.html

Scitech – Scitech website (2023), sourced in March 2024 from: https://www.scitech.org.au/about/

"*Spinners Hostel for Backpackers*" (2022) material sourced in March 2024 from website:
https://www.spinnershostel.com.au/

"*The Pullman, Bunker Bay*" (2023) material sourced from *All Accor* website, accessed on 3rd Feb 2024 from website:

The Museum of Western Australia - sourced from: https://visit.museum.wa.gov.au/boolabardip

"*Wadjemup, Rottnest Island Western Australia*" (2021) information sourced from the Rottnest Island Website in February: https://www.rottnestisland.com/

Western Publishing (2008-2023) *Margaret River Region*. material sourced in March 2024 from: https://www.margaretriverwesternaustralia.com.au/locations/margaret-river-region

Western Australia's Art Gallery. Material sourced in March 2024 from: https://www.visitacity.com/en/perth/itineraries/perth-in-one-day-easy-going-itinerary-day-1

Welcome to the Swan Valley (2023). Information sourced in March 2024 from: https://www.swanvalley.com.au/about-the-valley/welcome-to-the-swan-valley

What to pack for Perth (2023). Material sourced in March 2024 from: https://www.smartertravel.com/pack-perth-packing-list/

READ OTHER TRAVEL BOOKS FROM CZYK PUBLISHING

Travel Like a Local- Chicago

Travel Like a Local- Istanbul

Travel Like a Local- Milwaukee

Travel Like a Local- Orlando

Travel Like a Local- Denver

CZYKPublishing.com

GreaterThanaTourist.com

Printed by Amazon Italia Logistica S.r.l.
Torrazza Piemonte (TO), Italy